COMPARED TO WHAT?

Life and Times of a Detroit Musician

DAN LEWIS

with

SALLY SULFARO

where words connect

Advance Praise for
Compared to What?
Life and Times of a Detroit Musician

"Music has been a driving force in Danny Lewis' life for more than 40 years. His early career as a Detroit percussionist led him to the music scene, the late night clubs and even to the Detroit Jazz Festival. His lifelong passion is promoting music and the arts in all ways great and small. His sharp insight and wide-ranging appreciation of modern music is fully on display in this engrossing new book. Danny's contributions to the music world are even more inspiring given his challenge of life with cerebral palsy. His story is a testimony to resiliency."

—*Luis E. Torregrosa, M.D. (Detroit)*
Musicologist and jazz historian

"Besides being a lifelong friend of mine, Dan has earned a place in the fabric of the Detroit, national and international music community. His personality has touched a staggering number of people from all walks of life. His knowledge of jazz and most popular music is second to none. I'm glad Sal and Dan got to put this story together."

—*Dan Oestrike (Detroit)*
Arranger, producer, band leader and songwriter
Multi-genre bass guitarist who has toured,
recorded and performed with Detroit's top bands and
musicians including Luis and Mario Resto and co-founded
the 70s rock band Scott with Derek St. Holmes

"Music is the foundation of my relationship with Dan, the substance that has allowed our friendship to grow over the years. We've experienced many live world class performances together, and not one of them has disappointed because Dan chose them. He's always spot on when recommending great music. Our friendship, actually a brotherhood, is built on a shared passion for percussion. Dan is quite the jazz historian, and I've learned much of what I know about it from him."

—Ray Portugal (San Francisco)
Percussionist and multi-instrumentalist

"I'll always remember going with Dan to hear Elvin Jones at Orchestra Hall in Detroit. We went backstage afterward and waited for Elvin and his wife Keiko. Since he is from the Detroit area, many of Elvin's relatives were also waiting to greet him. When he walked in, he saw Dan and immediately exclaimed 'Dan' and rushed to him to give him a big hug! He wanted to make sure Dan had a ride home. I've never known anyone like Dan. To say that he hasn't allowed physical challenges to get in his way is an understatement. He not only loves music but also goes the extra mile to know all the facts down to recording sessions and record deals, going even further to seek out and befriend the artists themselves. His knowledge and passion for music is unsurpassed...to the extent that many, many musicians of various genres call to talk music, bounce ideas off him and listen to what he has to say. I do the same, but it goes beyond that with Dan and me. For 30 years, he has been one of my best friends and confidants. I love you, Dan!"

—Mark Moultrup (St. Petersburg, Florida)
Pianist, composer, arranger and producer

"In concert with the dynamic persona that is Dan Lewis, our friendship has evolved and continues to inspire a genuinely positive, spiritually driven, creative vibe in this life. It was during a vodka-fueled slugfest that I discovered there's a person with a harder head than my own...Danny Lewis...and that person has a mean left cross! Danny is a champion among men and, in a truly selfless way, has been driven to leave the world better than he found it. As we are hopefully becoming more mature, life's challenges create ramps that are increasingly steep to climb. In Dan's case, it seems to be a perpendicular ascent. Yet somehow he forges ahead and never looks back. I know that I'm a much better person by knowing Dan."

—Alan Ayoub (Detroit)
Multi-instrumentalist, composer, arranger and band leader
who has performed with the Detroit Symphony Orchestra
and many famous artists of various genres
Studio consultant for notables including Eminem and Dr. Dre

Dedicated to my parents,
Chuck and Suzanne Lewis
~~~and~~~
In memory
of my brother and confidant
Ron Smith of The Spinners
&
Scott Sulfaro,
blues man and music historian

Contents

Note from Dan Lewis about the book title: xiii

Foreword by Larry Fratangelo xix

There and Back by co-author Sally Sulfaro xxi

ONE: *Dreaded Crossroad* 1

TWO: *Rehearsals* 4

THREE: *Up & Down the Staircase* 29

FOUR: *Elusive Expectations* .38

FIVE: *Hallowed Ground, Scorched Earth* 57

SIX: *Escapades & Escapes* 77

SEVEN: *Avalon* 91

EIGHT: *Are You Listening?* 110

NINE: *Dissonance* 117

TEN: *Blind Alleys* 139

ELEVEN: *My Vinyl Temple* 152

TWELVE: *Mama Said There'd Be Days Like This* 161

            Narrative by Leonard King, Jr.

THIRTEEN: *Melody & Harmony* 175

FOURTEEN: *Morphing the Molecules* .206

Afterword by Dan Lewis. 212

Homage. 220

Index 236

Ending Note. 257

Note from Dan Lewis about the book title:

Compared to What? was chosen because so many people live in a consensus reality, accepting versions of truth presented by prevailing voices and neglecting their inner compasses. It keeps psychologists in business. There's little consideration of reality on a broader comparative scale. The title evokes personal reflection. I deal with situations on my terms, looking at life through my own lens and disregarding narratives from those who would tell me the way things are. People are strengthened by their own interpretations, arriving at their own conclusions, convictions and choices—not by group think. Independence of choice engenders personal freedom and self-trust, leading ultimately to the right decisions for oneself. My inner voice says, "Why should I listen to so many others about the ways of the world? Why should I blindly accept what is so widely peddled?" I'll find my own truth rather than buy into the half-baked wisdom that too often dominates the landscape. It isn't valid, and I reject it.

Book title based on the song "Compared to What,"
music and lyrics by Eugene (Gene) McDaniels,
recorded and performed by Les McCann and Eddie Harris
at the Montreux Jazz Festival, Switzerland, 1969,
and recorded by Roberta Flack, 1969

Two years into the writing of this book:

Damn it, man, let's get this book done! I'm living with reels running in my head.

♫

Three and a half years into the writing of this book as it's reaching completion:

The Pandemic

I find myself in a weird place. The world is in the throes of a pandemic, and I'm experiencing many uncertainties. Memories of my grandfather are flooding into my consciousness. He told me that after the Great Depression and again after World War II, people were unsure if their lives would ever be the same as before. There were bread lines and contagions such as tuberculosis and polio. Grandpa showed me around the ghetto in the 1960s with a purpose, opening my eyes to the state of humanity and how fortunate I was. It not only raised my awareness of realities, but seeing it also expanded my perspective and made me a survivor.

I don't know where the Covid-19 pandemic will take us, but I hope musicians will eventually be able to get back to what they've always known and the venues that allowed them to survive. Economic stability will follow the virus and in the opposite direction. I'm very hopeful that will be the case. Personally, I'll be forever changed. What Joni Mitchell wrote in "Big Yellow Taxi" comes to mind, that you don't realize what you have until it's gone. For everyone on the planet, it might necessitate existing within a new normal. I'm resolved to live in the moment and to be grateful for the day.

Culture War, Political Conflict and Social Upheaval

This is my view from the cheap seats, hoping the generations who have enjoyed freedom all their lives are aware of what it took to get here. The word *inalienable* doesn't mean that American freedoms and rights are necessarily ours to keep forever. It has been said that most human conflicts have been between the haves and the have-nots. This applies not only to money and material goods but also to privilege and equal justice under the law. Who is in charge and what keeps them there? George Carlin's humor was packed with truth. He spoke about the owners of the U.S.A.—corporations and the people who run them. In their self-absorbed, greedy minds, their needs and goals supersede the needs and even the survival of the masses. As Carlin said, "It's a big club, and you ain't in it." The club of the few at the top is big in the sense that its power and impact are far reaching. If there's one overarching threat to the republic and democracy, it's that club which has created a plutocracy—and our complacency in allowing it.

We seem to be at a teetering point these days, and I don't know where it will take us. I just know there are different types of dictators and that all of them would be happy to give us, the diverse collective, what they believe we deserve. In many ways, that has already happened and continues to happen. What makes this picture complicated is that people's perspectives, indeed their perceptions of truth and fiction, have been deliberately blurred, dividing us. Views are skewed in one direction or the other based on different cultures and life situations—and depending on whose words you choose to believe.

When it comes to activism, responses to injustice and people taking to the streets, I've seen it before in the 1960s during the race riots and protests against the Vietnam War. What concerns me now is the purposeful blurring of truth, and I'm alarmed by the number of citizens who are receptive to obvious false-hoods. Fingers are pointing in all directions, creating confusion and disunity as this book is being completed. Elvis Costello got it right in the song "Peace Love and Understanding." Who is to be trusted?

As memoirs go, this book is written in a non-traditional format. It is not recorded from start to finish in chronological order.

Dan's recall is often prompted by a recording or a song title. His life experiences, thoughts, beliefs and insights have been clustered into chapters according to themes. Chapter Seven: Avalon provides foundational information about Dan's early life and his family, a flashback of sorts.

Some terms and places are marked with an asterisk (*).
They are described and defined in an index
at the end of the book.

Foreword

Musician, music aficionado, discographer, gatekeeper of the art, friend and brother. These are the words I use to describe my colleague and cohort, Dan Lewis.

Always an adventure, the memorable times we shared together were, and are, the gifts of our journey—so much of life experienced within the aura of music. The groove, the pulse, the rhythm, the soul of music—it is what we sought. Like young lions on the hunt, we hungered for great music. We explored the magic of rhythm, melody and harmony.

Music was our muse, our mistress, luring us deeper and deeper into her loving embrace. We pursued her and experienced the many facets of her ubiquitous presence in people of all cultures and beliefs. She was always there for us, to accompany us as we experienced this life we are blessed with. And live music is what we craved. Like voyeurs, we glimpsed her beauty through live music—the living spirit of the art itself performed by masters of the craft. Shamans riding the rhythms to the heavens.

Like sponges, we absorbed the performances of some of the greatest musicians ever to walk the planet. We lived the "magic moments" that are "on the wind," unrecorded, only to be heard at that moment—the mystery of an ensemble becoming one glorious voice in its realization of a composition, the true joy and magic of live performance—all part of the sumptuous, ever-changing smorgasbord we know as music. Her many personalities, diverse culturally and musically, all speak our language—the universal language—the language of music.

In Time,

Larry Fratangelo

There and Back

There was no epiphany, no precipitating event, that inspired the writing of this book. The notion that Dan Lewis should tell his story had been lingering in my heart and mind for a long time. The circle of life can be traumatic, shaken by tragedy and loss, but fate feels less imposing if you stare it squarely in the face. Experiencing profound sorrow in my own life, I looked Dan up twenty-four years after meeting him, hoping to stare into the face of destiny with this intrepid man, a musician with a compelling narrative—a life with many stories that should be told.

It was in music venues in and around Detroit in the early '90s that I was introduced to Dan by bass guitarist Dan Oestrike and our sons, Abe and Josh Sulfaro, a.k.a. James and Michael Simmons of the James Michael Simmons Band. One quickly discerns that Dan is engaged in an ongoing, pithy dialogue with the world around him, a cyclorama of music, hopes, dreams and heart-wrenching negotiation with reality. To delve into a conversation with him is to be touched by an earthbound mystic and hence my return to this enduring conversation with him after so many years. As you read, you'll note that even though I've referred to Dan in terms that aptly describe his ability to peer into and beyond realities, he's no saint. In fact, some of the stories herein reveal the gritty, earthy and rebel-prone aspects of his character.

Dan's words on January 18, 2017 during the first interview for his autobiography: "As sad as I feel about what's going on in my life right now, there's still my music...always music...and my will." At the time of this statement, Dan resides in an assisted living facility in downriver Detroit. Until three years ago, his mother, Suzanne, helped him with activities of daily living. When she developed Alzheimer's disease and became incapable of caring for an adult son with cerebral palsy, he was forced to find another place to live. It is from a place of deep sadness and loss that Dan is speaking, finding himself without Suzanne's abiding presence. His best friend and lifelong advocate has become absent.

Residents of the assisted living facility have vacated the dining area after lunch when my husband, Michael, and I arrive. The large room is empty except for two stragglers at the far end near the wall, one of them in a wheelchair. Dan's profile is unmistakable even though I haven't seen him in over two decades. Hair now graying, he's otherwise unchanged. As we approach, I gratefully note the powerful, stirring aura that still emanates from him as he recognizes us—and the same soulful vibration that I remember around this man. His magnetic persona remains intact, and again I sense a resolve that is not passively inherited through one's DNA but rather brewed and steeped during years of daily challenges, disappointments and unfulfilled dreams while chasing dreams up mountains. And of course, there's Dan's own brand of joy and infectious laughter.

This is an anthology, a compendium of the thoughts and experiences of a hard-driven percussionist and music aficionado with a dauntless spirit. Dan tells his life story at times with a crusty edge and at other times with sensitivity and gentle wisdom. He also reveals unhappiness and unrealized dreams in transparent fashion, emanating a tough but tender vibe. You'll turn the last page knowing Dan Lewis not only as a musician's musician but also as a remarkable human being who lives as he speaks, makin' it real but also demanding that music be as close as possible to an ideal.

During the writing of this book, there have been times when Dan's angst and ardor have marched headlong into Lenny Bruce territory. He shares this memoir and his views on music and the world in unpolished prose akin to a beat poet. There's no mistaking who's on the phone when he calls. "Sal, dig." It's been an enlightening trip, Dan, a rough ride at times but a trip I'm honored to have shared with you.

Sally Sulfaro

Dan Lewis with his band Dan Lewis and Friends,
1994 Trenton MI Jazz Festival

CHAPTER ONE
Dreaded Crossroad

Bittersweet memories...my mind meandering back through the years...vivid recollections of parents who cut me no slack because of my disability, who sent me to a psychologist so that I could learn how to play with others, memories of Mom in the role of late night chauffeur as she loaded my gear in and out of cabs and transported me to and from practice sessions and performances, bribing me to do my homework with the promise of a trip to Crown Drugstore at the corner of Fort Street and Fort Park where vinyl records were sold, and the many occasions when our home was opened to musicians, musicians, and more musicians including Elvin Jones, Rod Stewart, Mark Murphy, Parliament-Funkadelic and Dave Liebman.

So this is it, the dreaded moment I knew would come except when I was a kid. The young live in the moment. Children don't fret about what the future holds, even after they're old enough to know that heartaches and death are inevitable. My mom Suzanne kept it real, lovingly preparing me for life outside the mainstream. She sometimes released me into the world unsheltered, allowing me to see for myself that it would be a difficult journey and hoping to make me aware that I'd never have a regular life.

Looking back now, Mom was right about so many things. The women I've been involved with, even though I met most of them through music and in music venues, ultimately didn't understand the heart and soul of a musician. Most of them weren't willing to stay on the journey with me. Even if they were willing, there wasn't enough room in my life for a third party alongside my mistress and my religion, music. "Danny, there will never be a woman who can compete with music, including me. You'll never love a woman as much as you love music." I hear Suzanne's voice as if she's speaking to me in present time. Precious scenes flood my mind, tears welling up from deep places as I sit at my mother's bedside. This brilliant woman is the pillar of my existence, my best friend and advocate...always.

Mom understood that I was on a mission to share the gift of music with others when I was a child. She crossed lines for me in the 1960s when neighbors in Lincoln Park thought she was neglectful, even downright negligent, for allowing me to slow-crawl around the block with pads on my knees and a transistor radio tied around my neck. I could maneuver myself around much better then, in and out of my bed and wheelchair. I was trying to get to know the kids in the neighborhood and share the gift that meant so much to me. I would soon learn that they didn't care to know me or receive the gift that I was attempting to deliver. To them, I must have looked like an alien, and perhaps I was. Some of the kids literally threw stones. One of the neighbors brought me home in a shopping cart. "He's in danger!" Mom blew them off numerous times. In her own way, Suzanne Lewis told them to go pound sand. They underestimated her judgment and the kid who they thought needed to be coddled and protected. She'd let me go out again and again—with a watchful eye. She knew what she was doing, and she knew me.

When you begin to see the possibilities of music, you desire to do something really good for people.... I want to speak to their souls.
John Coltrane

Mom started baking cookies to entice kids to come inside and listen to music that didn't interest them. Once inside our house, in spite of my efforts to keep them listening, they filled their pockets with cookies as they headed for the door. Only Suzanne understood the power of music in my life, how my spirit rose up out of my body when I heard Coltrane's *A Love Supreme. She didn't underestimate me, and she didn't take credit years later when those same neighbors showed up to see me on stage with well known Detroit musicians at the Wyandotte Art Fair. They told her, "It's wonderful what you've done." She responded, "I didn't do it. This is who Dan is."

Damn, she's awesome, the consummate mother on a sacred mission, one compounded by challenges and heartaches that push limits beyond what most could endure—having two children with cerebral palsy—me and my sister Lori. Watching Suzanne slip away over the past few years, her brilliance, actually her essence, gradually stolen by Alzheimer's disease, has given me time to contemplate the inevitable, this dreaded crossroad. Life will never be the same, but there's still music and my will, the will that she nurtured in me. Suzanne, Mom, I'm still tapping into the indelible imprint of your spirit upon mine, hearing refrains of *A Love Supreme and your comforting guidance in whatever I do.

CHAPTER TWO
Rehearsals

Man, sometimes it takes you a long time to sound like yourself.
Miles Davis

I wasn't popular with the neighborhood kids, not only because of my disability but also because my interests didn't align with theirs. It's no wonder my parents and the child psychologists said I needed to learn to play with others. If neighborhood kids came into our house to visit, what did I do? I remained buried in the pile of 45s that were strewn around me and continued the records I was playing, not going out of my way to interact with them unless they were willing to enter the dimension where I existed. Perhaps our disconnect was in the meaning of the word "play."

Music was what I needed most, but it led me to a lonely place. My passion for it gave Chuck and Suzanne Lewis a powerful behavior modification tool that was used when I crossed lines, and I crossed many. All it usually took to get me to toe the line was the threat of keeping me from a performance either on stage or in the audience. As I grew old enough to be out in the city by myself, the quest for music and a relentless drive for the life of a musician sometimes beckoned me to unsafe places. At the end of an evening, Clarence Baker (*Baker's Keyboard Lounge) used to wheel me past hookers and junkies to the Top Hat, a burger joint where I'd wave down a cab for a ride home. I think my mom and dad reached a point where they realized that my life circumstances were hardship enough without the constraints and social suffocation that their protectiveness would impose, so they allowed me to experience life and didn't shelter me. I was permitted to strike out into the world on my own terms. I used to hitch-hike alone in a wheelchair in the '70s—fearless to a fault. Whatever will be, will be.

I'll play it first and tell you what it is afterwards.
Miles Davis

The life rehearsals were many, but I didn't realize at the time that the situations and people of my childhood and early adulthood were practice sessions placed before me for reasons that I've now come to appreciate. I never liked the circus and the clowns, and so many early experiences were filled with activities and characters of that type—Pollyanna, Bozo the Clown and Mary Poppins—irritating, like happy face stickers intended to keep your mindset sunny and, worst of all, superficial. Too often I took the path of least resistance and settled for the role of people pleaser, coloring inside the lines. But in the end, it didn't matter how submissive and agreeable I was. People weren't convinced by my half-hearted attempts at doing what was expected, and I was left holding my dick. It's not that I'm opposed to compromise, but negotiation seldom yields complete satisfaction for the parties involved. I don't believe I've been rebellious or contrarian merely for the sake of being difficult; I just haven't had options in many situations because of my physical limitations. In some instances, I decided to voice my objections firmly or rebel outright. It has never been clear whether the things I got into trouble for as a child were related to my detachment from the mainstream or if I was a kid who would have questioned norms and defiantly ignored them in any life circumstance. My sense is that it was both.

Painful Truths

Dad sends everyone to bed early on Christmas Eve 1965, telling us we'll need to get a good night's sleep because Santa Claus will be leaving presents for us to open when we wake up in the morning. This doesn't sit well with me because I want to watch Andy Williams on TV, so of course I don't go to sleep. Shortly before midnight, I hear paper rustling and Mom and Dad talking softly. At seven years of age, I'm nimble, able to quietly lift myself from bed to wheelchair. From a vantage point where I'm not seen, I peek around a corner and see Dad placing packages under the tree and munching on the cookies that my sister left out for Santa.

Reality and folklore can be trouble-prone companions in the mind of a child. The discovery that Santa Claus is a fraud triggers a plan by me, self-appointed agent of truth, to share this shocker with the kids at school. To me, it's simple. What is real is real, and what isn't isn't. The truth must be told. And why limit the message to Santa? What about the Tooth Fairy and the Easter Bunny? The kids at school will bring in their presents to show them off at the first show 'n tell after Christmas break, so it's the perfect time to share my discovery. Of course my classmates will want to know about this!

I deliver the public service announcement and wait for jaws to drop open in astonishment. Jaws drop all right, but not out of surprise. Some kids have quivering chins, and others cry openly. Santa Claus and other childhood folklore are no big deal to me, but apparently they are a big deal to the other kids. Uh oh...I'm the one who gets an eye-opener. I've stripped Superman of his cape, and my buddy Mark Conti is laughing his ass off in the back row.

I'm sent to the principal's office for a come-to-Jesus meeting about my blasphemy, and I'm suspended for a week. At home, my mom and dad get phone calls from the parents of my classmates who say I've ruined their children's enjoyment of the holidays. Dad slides into disciplinarian mode, and I'm given an ultimatum. "Tell 'em you saw Rudolph on the roof, damn it! Tell 'em Santa slid down our chimney! You will apologize to your classmates, or you won't be performing at the *Wisdom Tooth with Vernor Highway Blues Band."

When I return to school, a note is delivered to me in class: Report to the principal's office. I've been hoping the interaction with Mr. Behm on the day of my transgression was the end of it, but he doesn't drop it that easily. The only behavior modification that had hit home was the threat of having my music activities curtailed by my parents, so this follow-up counseling session with the principal triggers another type of epiphany for me. He tells me, "The next time you have something to share, remember that your information isn't necessarily appropriate for your classmates. Everyone will be better off if you keep subjects that are unsuitable for children to yourself. There's no need to share everything that's on your mind." He must be reading my thoughts because he continues, "If you don't agree with what I'm telling you, you'll just have to go along to get along." At this moment, I know that I'll never convince anyone here at school of anything that I believe is important or relevant, even when I think they need to know it.

Looking back now, the principal was right. The more I pushed what I believed were important perspectives, the more I learned to keep quiet. Regardless of which parent drew the line on my misbehaviors, lines were drawn and childhood behaviors were kept within boundaries...most of the time. In hindsight, it's clear that I was never really a kid. I had to exist within a space that was hemmed in not only by physical limitations but also personal expectations that weren't aligned with a traditional childhood environment. To this day, I wonder if any of my classmates required therapy because of the psychological trauma inflicted on them by the evil kid who smashed their childhood fantasies.

Farm Fiascos

On a school field trip to a farm, we go into the barn where the farmer asks, "Have you guys ever milked a cow?" Despite my age (6 or 7 years), I'm thinking I've already had enough of this Romper Room jive and would rather be at home listening to music. I'm in a pushcart, and they've placed me at the front where I can see, so it's conspicuous when he asks for a volunteer and I don't raise my hand. The teachers are constantly encouraging me to participate like a good boy, based on the psychologist's recommendations. Of course I'm chosen.

Leaning over the side of the pushcart and following the farmer's instructions, I place my hands on the cow's udders, squeeze and pull downward toward the bucket. As if she has been waiting for this ridiculous exercise in elementary education, the cow turns her rear end toward me, raises her tail and pees in a torrent that only a huge cow can produce. I can't exactly dodge the yellow stream. It's a hot day, and I don't have a change of clothes, so I'm wet, smelly and plagued by flies for the remainder of the outing. The kids hold their noses and keep their distance from me on the bus all the way back to school.

Dad takes me horseback riding. They lift me up on the horse's back, and my father gives the horse a smack on the rear to get it moving. Instead moving forward in a walking gait, the horse lunges. I'm thrown off, landing under the horse, and it steps on my chest. After determining that I'm not seriously injured, the woman who works here instructs my father, "Put him back up on the horse now, or he'll never want to get on a horse again." Hearing what she's saying, I yell, "Bullshit! I'm not getting back on a horse now or ever."

Even as a young child, I know I don't need the Roy Rogers stuff. It seems to make everybody happy except me. I'm expected to take part in activities that well meaning people think I should experience. As I grow older, I go along to get along, allowing them to take me to unwanted activities, games and outings, all the while thinking, "This stuff doesn't work for me. No apple orchard visits, no circus, no petting zoos, please. Do you even know me? Enough participation in activities that I don't choose. No more farms." I don't even like milk. I drink coffee even as a kid. I'm all about farms and the food they produce for all of us, but just throw some fast food from a chain restaurant at me and I'm good. Horses are beautiful to look at, but I prefer concrete under my wheels and the smell of an occasional updraft from city sewers.

Shhh!

Even though I'm only eight years old, our neighbor Janie Peters understands how serious I am about music and becoming a drummer. She takes me to drum lessons at Town and Country, a record store in Lincoln Park, and she listens when I practice. I hip Janie to the great R&B artists including Major Lance and Curtis Mayfield as well as obscure soul music on radio, WCHB-AM and WJLB-AM.

While sitting with me for my parents, Janie introduces me to folk songs by Joan Baez, Bob Dylan, Buffy Sainte-Marie, Woody Guthrie, Gordon Lightfoot and Joni Mitchell—music so mesmerizing that I ask her to keep quiet when the music is playing. "No talking, please! Listen to this." She goodheartedly laughs at me. I love the melodies in folk music but also its word art. This is when I learn the importance of the stories in folk music. I ask Janie to explain the meaning of each song—after it finishes playing, of course. The meanings feed my imagination and relax me. I tell her that I'm going to be a musician and surround myself in vinyl for the rest of my life.

I subject all my sitters to a firm insistence on quiet when we're playing records because I'm an intense listener. I start watching shows like Hootenanny and begin listening to the Kingston Trio, Pete Seeger and Peter, Paul and Mary.

Shifting World Axis

I meet 19-year-old Dave Greene, harmonica player and singer, in 1965 through my cousin, 18-year-old Bob Higgins who's the organist and saxophonist in a group Dave formed, the Vernor Highway Blues Band. Over the next three years, my world expands. They play real blues—the music of Paul Butterfield and Muddy Waters.

I dig the downtrodden themes. After showing up at their practice sessions a few times, Dave and Bob take me on as a band member, playing tambourine and maracas. Vernor Highway Blues Band provides an escape from the purgatory of school. I'm a fan of Junior Parker and Big Joe Turner, not to mention having a bad case of real-life blues, so I can relate to music about hard times. A psychologist at school, probably the one who suggested that I learn to play with others, asks me about my less-than-sunny interests, "Why are you always pushing boundaries?" My answer: "Because I need real. I have to deal with sheltered, happy-talk Pollyannas at school." At this tender age, the music played by Vernor Highway helps me connect with life in a way that pretend cowboys and Indians can't.

Then a seismic event takes place. Knowing that I idolize Charlie Watts (Rolling Stones) and Sam Lay (Paul Butterfield Blues Band), Bob tells me, "You ain't heard nothin' yet. You're gonna hear a real drummer!" He carries me upstairs to his apartment and puts on a Coltrane record, "My Favorite Things." To say that I immediately get hip to Coltrane would be a serious understatement, and hearing the legendary drumming of native Detroiter Elvin Jones for the first time—pure joy. My connection with music is forever changed in the best possible way.

> Coltrane's tone is beautiful because it's functional.
> In other words, it is always involved in saying something.
> You can't separate the means that a man uses to
> say something from what he ultimately says.
> Technique is not separated from its content in a great artist.
> *Cecil Taylor*

I have no interest in the teeny-bopper crap that's playing on radio stations. I'm looking for higher ground, and Bob becomes my gateway to elevated music sensibilities. It's because of him that I receive a blessing that's also a curse—elitist ideals about music. Only a Mercedes will do, never a Ford Pinto. Emulate the masters, no Top 40 shit. Bob single-handedly inspires me to dedicate myself to the muse and grow within the art, leading me to discernment that will endure for the rest of my life. He exposes me to the finest live music available at venues that include the *Grande Ballroom, *The 20 Grand, Fox Theater, the *Chess Mate, *The Livingroom, *Baker's Keyboard Lounge, the *Grand Riviera Theater, *Ethel's Cocktail Lounge, *Dummy George's, *Morey Baker's and *Eastown Theatre. We attend live performances by Laura Nyro, Paul Butterfield, Sam & Dave, Roberta Flack, Cream, Blood Sweat & Tears, Les McCann, Herbie Mann, Monty Alexander and José Feliciano performing with Paulinho Da Costa. After each concert, I record a summary of the event, a critical review of sorts, made possible by a Sony stereo reel-to-reel that my dad bought for me. I'm serious in this endeavor, but Bob thinks it's funny. The recordings provide material for show 'n tell at school—not that any information about music would interest my classmates or make the teachers more tolerant of my total immersion. My recordings include reviews of The Doors, Janis Joplin and a compelling, pivotal artist named Jimi Hendrix who is showing how far boundaries can be stretched. For me, it's like a journal, a way to express myself.

Bob brings musicians from across Detroit to my house for jam sessions and holds Vernor Highway practices here. One of the most touching and inspiring musicians he brings to visit is a young man named David Lasley who is auditioning for a part in the musical *Hair* at the Vest Pocket Theatre in Birmingham. His soprano voice blows me away—like a nightingale, such a special artist, songwriter and singer. Sitting crossed-legged on our living room floor, he plays reel-to-reel tapes in stereo and shares the insights of someone trying to break into the business in L.A. It's apparent he'll make his way, and he does, becoming a back-up singer for James Taylor and many other well known artists. He's a featured back-up singer on James Taylor Online, Taylor describing his voice as "angelic." David has also recorded several solo albums.

I study the recordings of Chicago blues artists Howlin' Wolf, Paul Butterfield, James Cotton, Lightnin' Hopkins and Little Walter Jacobs. I learn about meter and keeping time, absorbing every concept and new skill with voracity, driven by a dream and unhappiness with my life and school. Vernor Highway Blues Band provides my first stage experiences at Detroit area music venues such as the *Chess Mate, *Grande Ballroom and a 60s hippie haven called the *Wisdom Tooth at the corner of Plum and 5th Streets. We perform tunes by Howlin' Wolf and Muddy Waters on stages shared with the Lovin' Spoonful and the early Bee Gees.

Dave and Bob, through their sensitivity and compassion as well as sweet providence, become my immediate family. Dave understands my anger and discontent. He listens and provides an outlet for intermittent escape. He interprets the stories that live in blues lyrics, encouraging me to transfer those emotions to my instruments. Beyond that, Dave shows me love and kindness, helping me see purpose in each day and move toward a higher consciousness, particularly through writer and poet Della Doan, the spiritually gifted mother of his guitarist friend Millard Doan. Before Bob gets his own apartment, I sometimes stay at his family's house downtown. His mother, Polly, looks after me when I'm there. During the race riots, the National Guard can be seen patrolling the area. One night in 1967, we're scheduled to play at the *Wisdom Tooth, but it's burned by rioters who are setting the Motor City on fire.

Looking back now, I realize that I was a kid who needed to validate my life. The years with Vernor Highway Blues Band and my friendship with Bob Higgins and Dave Greene gave me hope and a destination. It will always amaze me that two teenagers took me under their wings and welcomed me into their band and their lives. The time with them impacted my life as an aspiring percussionist and as a human being grappling with harsh reality and the meaning of life. In the years since, Dave has come to my gigs and has even been a guest performer. With him on harmonica and vocals at the Trenton Theater, we did an encore that brought the house down with a rousing rendition of Fleetwood Mac's classic "Stop Messin' Round."

Their Trash, My Treasure

"Why do you do this? Don't bring your trash music to school again. It's upsetting." I've been scolded, embarrassed and threatened into understanding that, once again, I've been a wrecking ball at weekly show 'n tell. My classmates bring in their coloring books and tadpoles in a jar, but for me the lyrics of Billy Strayhorn's jazz standard "Lush Life" provide meaningful insights into another kind of experience—crusty dives and lives gone wrong. The teacher says my music is depressing and inappropriate for kids my age, so I decide to let it blow over for a few weeks before persisting in my attempts to deliver an unwanted gift.

The final reckoning comes when I bring in a Ray Charles record, "Hey Now." To kick off my presentation, believing real life is reflected in the song, I tell the class, "Dig this! This *cat has a story to tell." It doesn't occur to me that the term "cat" probably misleads the kids into expecting a cartoon character like Felix. I play the record, Ray singing a sad song about love gone bad, rubbing the empty pillow next to him and feeling so awful he could just die. Without missing a beat when the song ends, I add the biographical information about Ray's life including the unsavory facts that have since become widely known because of the movie *Ray*. The expressions on my classmates' faces range from cluelessness to shock and disbelief. There are no looks of interest or pleasant surprise. What immediately takes place is a replay of the incident when I pronounced Santa Claus a fraud. Another call is made to my parents.

There's one teacher in particular who gives me a ration of shit about my music, but ironically she and I both dig the folk group Peter, Paul and Mary. For me, it's only because I'm in love with Mary Travers and her long, blonde hair. Their songs are mostly syrupy and silly, definitely not hip. Even when given the honor of singing "Day Is Done" with Paul Stuckey at the Muscular Dystrophy Telethon, I thought how lame the song is and was tempted to get my hip hammer out and use it on him. But back to the teacher, she's battling demons. One day she unravels, her face twitching and contorting. The entire class watches, aghast and whimpering, as she's taken away by guys in white jackets—another traumatic experience for my sheltered classmates. As she's being removed, I wheel myself to the back of the classroom, sharing nervous laughter with my classmate Mark Conti who also has cerebral palsy. He says to me, "Can't you just wait 'til the day you and I can get the fuck out of here?"

1967 and 1968 are prickly school years for me. I finally accept the fact that what's catnip to me is unsettling to my classmates, and it's not just the music that upsets kids and teachers. It's also the subject of the occult that I'm exposed to by my grandfather that scares them (Chapter 7: Avalon, section Tragic and Magic). To avoid discipline at home, I stop participating in show 'n tell and sit politely and silently through weekly displays of gerbils running on wheels, stories of make-believe and autographed pictures of Bozo the Clown as my rejection of the school scene grows. At this point, I'm thinking, "Fuck Bozo."

I was always doing revolutionary things, things that would alert people, so they would stop being so subservient.
Charles Mingus

I now wonder if I was trying to stick it to kids who lived in a parallel universe, having nothing in common with me except their age. I just wanted to listen to music and play the drums. My records were my world, my comfort. They transported me to an alternate reality, a place where no one was throwing stones at the alien kid with a transistor radio. When I was in school, I daydreamed, all the while saying "yes" to Thelonius Monk and "no" to school. I longed for a different kind of classroom. There's little wonder that I was sent to a psychologist to learn how to play with others. I didn't have that inclination, and why should I? They weren't interested in listening to great music with me, so why should I want to play with them? I lived on a musical playground with Paul Butterfield and Muddy Waters. I never finished high school.

Get yourself out of whatever cage you find yourself in.
John Cage

All these years later, former classmates occasionally invite me to reunions and dinners to catch up on each other's lives and, of course, to reminisce. I politely decline because I have no desire to revisit those unpleasant years and memories of days spent in a place where I didn't want to be. Mark Conti and I ran into one of our elementary school teachers, Mrs. Okey, at the mall about forty years after we were in her class. Her first name was Ann. We used to call her Annie Oakley. She asked, "What are you doing with yourself these days?" When I told her I'm a musician, she replied, "No surprise. You used to drive me nuts with the constant drumming on your desk." I told her, "I don't do it for free anymore. You'd have to go to a night club and pay to hear me."

Task Master

I form a band without a name in 1970, and we practice in the family room at my house. We're rehearsing for my dad's company picnic. The kids in the group subsist on a diet of pop music, so we play lame Top 10 hits like "96 Tears" by Question Mark and the Mysterians and "Walk Don't Run" by The Ventures. I'm pushing them to practice more so we'll be tight but also to expand our repertoire. I propose kicking it up with some Jeff Beck and Traffic tunes. Dan the task master, relentlessly on a quest for excellence even at the tender age of twelve. I'm always trying to do justice to a piece of music.

My goal is for the band perform well enough to get paid gigs in venues beyond birthday parties and backyard picnics. The other guys, however, have no goals related to music or the band. Like other 11- and 12-year-olds, they just want to have fun. During practice when I demand to repeat a tune in pursuit of a better arrangement, Mike Gilbert, the drummer, pushes back. He's just close enough for me to punch him in the face, losing my balance and almost falling off my stool. They tell me they're all going outside to ride their bikes, and they do, reducing me to tears.

The band plays at my dad's company picnic, but I'm not satisfied with our performance. I'm unreasonable, expecting too much, and the kids begin to avoid me. The unnamed band becomes a lonely pursuit—just me, a steadfast guitar player named Bob Ferraiuolo and a loyal drummer named Mike Gilbert, even after I punched him, hanging in there with me after the mutiny.

To this day, Bob and Mike are constants in my life. They're positive forces who share their troubles and joys with me, and I share mine with them.

Star Burst

Rod Stewart's voice is bluesy, pleasantly raspy, as he sings with The Jeff Beck Group. I love the sound of this artist and go to hear him whenever he's in town whether at the *Grande Ballroom, *Eastown Theater or *The Palladium (Birmingham). It's especially nice at the Grande where operator Russ Gibb gives me access to performers. I get acquainted with Rod after he leaves The Jeff Beck Group and joins Faces. We share an appreciation of Mississippi Delta blues singers: Sippie Wallace, Mississippi Fred McDowell, Sonny Boy Williamson, Little Walter Jacobs, Muddy Waters and Son House. We talk about our record collections.

"God damn, Dan! Can I borrow?" He calls from England, we talk blues, and we mail records back and forth.

One day my sister's friend, Rosalyn, answers the phone. When a man asks to speak to Dan, she asks, "May I ask who's calling?" "Rod Stewart." She begins squealing, "Oh, my God! Oh, my God! Dan! Dan! It's Rod Stewart!" He offers to come and get me for a performance, and when he shows up at the house, who else but Rosalyn answers the door. Repeat performance. The couple of years (1968-70) before superstar status consumes him, Rod is able to connect with me when he's in town. It's a time of great days and late nights. He puts me on stage, and sometimes, as corny as it is, he wheels me around in the middle of a song like a stage prop. It's during these years that I become aware of the girls, girls, girls who are atwitter over musicians. Rod's career soon skyrockets, and we lose touch.

Editorial comment: Rod's music quality took a dive when it became radio-ready with pop tunes such as "Every Picture Tells a Story" and "Maggie May." His earlier recordings with The Jeff Beck Group, Faces and on his solo albums were better in my opinion, but I've been late in understanding that art and enterprise have different purposes and different audiences.

The Ungrateful Fan

I'm 11 years old. Dad is with me at the Muscular Dystrophy Telethon that Jerry Lewis hosts each Labor Day at the *Americana Hotel in New York City. Jerry invites me every year. Most of the people at this event can't tell that I don't have muscular dystrophy. This year, they've set up a press room with lights, photographers and a film crew to do a promotional shoot with Joe Namath. I'm looking cool in bell bottoms and hippie clothes, and I get chosen to be in the shoot. My father, a sports fan, is envisioning a show 'n tell with his buddies because the prize is a football autographed by Joe and the Los Angeles Rams.

The event organizers are assuming that all boys are football fans, so no one is prepared for my response when Broadway Joe offers me the signed football. "No thanks. I'm not into football." Attempting to maintain the spirit of the giveaway and being unaware of my familiarity with his bio, Joe asks, "What are you into?" I tell him, "I'm a musician. I'd rather go to your nightclub, Bachelors III, and hear some live music." There are dumbstruck expressions across the room. Not waiting for Joe to respond, I add, "You host some great musicians there like Blood, Sweat and Tears. Or a ticket to a Rolling Stones, B.B. King or Count Basie performance would be awesome!" Jaws drop, and the camera crew can be heard chuckling. I continue, "And you're in that movie CC and Company. I'd like to see that, too, because I love Ann-Margaret. You're the luckiest man in the world. She's a real dish!" Joe laughs and says, "Dan, I have to agree with you. She really is." At this point, there's audible rustling and snickers. Then I tell Joe, "I'd like to hear about what goes on inside the Playboy Mansion, too." There's dismay on the faces of onlookers. The film crew is choking back laughter.

There's displeasure and disappointment on my dad's face, not only because of my cheeky behavior but even more so because he wanted that autographed football! He's giving me the look, furrowed eyebrows and a grimace, and I can tell he's suppressing the urge to whoop the tar out of me. What kid wouldn't want a football signed by Joe Namath and the L.A. Rams? The Muscular Dystrophy Association people can't wait to get me out of here, so they proceed with the photo op—Joe handing me the football that I've declined. Back in our room, Dad is livid, and we're empty handed. Joe didn't offer me a free pass to a performance at Bachelors III. I'm sure there's an age requirement at that establishment, but I also know he could make it happen regardless of my age.

♫

Some things never change. Many years later in 1994 on a plane between Chicago and Detroit, my girlfriend Jan is reading to me from Miles Davis' autobiography, *Miles* (1990). In Miles fashion, the words "fuck," "fucker" and "fucking" permeate the text. This seems to grab the attention of the man seated next to me. He inquires what the book is about, and I tell him as Jan holds it up for him to see the cover. Perhaps to change the subject, he asks what I do. I tell him I'm a musician, a percussionist. Not wanting to appear rude or disinterested, I ask what he does. He simply tells me he plays hockey. I ask if he plays on a league, and he replies, "Of sorts." He asks my name and I tell him. I ask his name and he says simply, "Steve."

There's a pleasant chemistry between us, and we delve into a conversation that covers several topics including a house he's building. I buy us a couple of drinks. As we're landing, Steve tells me, "Dan, I've really enjoyed talking to you. Would you like to come to a hockey game? I can get you some good tickets." I look to Jan and ask if she'd like to go to a game. She's not interested and tells us she'll probably have to work. I thank Steve for the offer and decline. I can sense that we're being watched and overheard, but I'm clueless as to why until we're deplaning and there's a cluster of press people and cameras at the gate. When Steve walks onto the jet bridge, a woman who was seated across the aisle from us says in a sharp tone, "Well! You really got some quality time with Steve Yzerman. I can't believe you didn't take him up on the tickets!"

Her words were kind compared to what my father, the sports fan, says when I tell him about meeting Steve Yzerman and the ticket offer. "God damn it! You did what? The Red Wings are hot! They're making history in the hockey world!" At this point, he's so upset and angry that I'm wondering if he'll kick me out of the house. "You've got to learn to be more grateful and accept complementary offers," he admonishes me.

As usual, I've been a lousy fan, but in this case, I didn't know I was interacting with hockey great Steve Yzerman. Even if I had recognized him, I wouldn't have known that the Detroit Red Wings were enjoying a highly publicized winning streak with Steve as captain because I don't follow sports. In spite of my dad's irritation at the time, he later entertained his friends with the story, laughing about how I probably broadened Yzerman's perspective during the most highly publicized time in his career. Even though I didn't know I was talking to a hockey world idol, I've learned that most famous people appreciate being allowed to be out of character without being fawned over, just regular folk among regular folk. If Yzerman had been a well known musician, I'd have recognized him right away. But even then, I don't gush. As far as the pleasant conversation with Steve, Jan and I joked that he was probably trying to interrupt the gritty language of Miles Davis.

Sweet Settling

It's the mid-70s and I'm a teenager who's longing to be a drummer, but I can't use the foot pedals. What kind of drummer can't deliver a full bass kick? As jazz improvisation compares to life, there's the familiar adage about what to do when life gives you lemons. How well can you solo within a composition that you wouldn't have chosen? This is my reality, life on a relative scale with constant negotiation and compromise.

Along comes a friendship with a master and, as has been the case in my life, Elvin Jones and sweet providence deliver guidance and encouragement at exactly the time it's needed. I tell him I've been thinking about East Indian rhythms, ragas, using finger drums called tablas even though my fingers are stiff and slow. Elvin thoughtfully responds with words I'll never forget. "Look man, just because your legs don't work doesn't mean your hands don't work. It's all African rhythm through your hands and upper body strength. You have a solid sense of timing and rhythm. Forget about tablas. You can use your hands with congas and other percussion instruments to accomplish your goal."

Lights begin flashing in my head. That settles it! Hand percussion—congas and small percussion. Thanks to Elvin, there's a newfound path forward. So begins my journey as a percussionist.

Elvin's warmth and sensitivity are shown again in 1993 when I take a musician friend, Mark Moultrup, backstage to meet him. Elvin greets me with a hug and asks who my friend is. Mark jokingly tells Elvin that I was hitchhiking and he picked me up. Elvin makes no indication that he heard the benign joke, probably an indication that he considers it distasteful. He immediately deflects by asking if I need a ride home, a kindness he has extended to me many times when he's playing in Detroit. To relieve the mutual discomfort, I tell Elvin about the Bennie Maupin project (Chapter 10: Blind Alleys, section The Dangling Project). As always, he and his wife Keiko (composer and arranger) are supportive and happy that I'm into it. Mark still laughs about the hitch-hiking comment.

Disqualified

I'm a 17-year-old hanging out with musicians—serious musicians. I'm into big band sounds influenced by Tower of Power, Chase, Duke Ellington and the Allman Brothers. There's going to be a talent competition at school, and I'm totally underwhelmed by the thin sounds produced by the groups that have entered the contest. When I inquire about entering the competition with a group I've put together, I'm told there's a limit of five or six musicians per group. This rule, set by the student council, runs up against my go-big-or-go-home fixation because I like BIG sound and because of my longstanding insecurity and a need to prove something, to show the world how awesome music can be. I'm reluctant and yet determined to enter the competition, knowing my preferences and plan aren't aligned with the contest rules. The truth is I can't even think of delivering anything less than a BIG music set with Afro-Cuban sounds woven in.

I lie on the application, listing six people in my band, and immediately begin layering the group by adding two keyboard players, three guitarists and three female singers. My hand percussion needs support but the drummer is weak, so I enlist the skills of Rudy Lopez, an Afro-Cuban percussionist. This brings the total to 11 people. We practice at my house for two or three weeks and by show date, we're tight. The musicians in my group are guarded about our prospects, some of them warning me, "You're pushing your luck, Dan." I respond, "Yeah, we're already in trouble."

Jazz is the big brother of revolution. Revolution follows it around.

Miles Davis

I'm still telling them to be cool as the curtain goes up. Amazingly, the judges allow us to perform two numbers, "Whipping Post" (Allman Brothers) and "Sympathy for the Devil" (Rolling Stones). In keeping with my premeditated defiance of the rules, we play past the time limit, but we receive a standing ovation. That's all I need, so I'm not a bit upset or disappointed when we're disqualified as expected. The rebel in me, who should have known better, tells the judges, "The music comes first, not the number of musicians." With this attitude, I've earned our elimination from the competition, but I leave the auditorium knowing the audience received one hell of a BIG performance. Even though I don't say it, I'm thinking rules are for fools. It's not like we had to win. Look at our performance!

The next day, our performance is the talk of the school, but the accolades don't prevent the principal from calling me to his office, elementary school *déjà vu*. "Why do you go against the grain? You just have to do things your way." He tells me not to do something like this again. It's clear that I won't be taking part in future talent shows. Me to myself: Oh well, the kids liked it, and we opened up broader possibilities. It's okay, not worth my while to participate again. High schools really don't want you to venture out into the frontier. You've just gotta chill inside their boundaries.

In retrospect, I more than pushed it when I entered the talent contest. As for school overall, I was always an outsider. I would have preferred to excel academically, but it was beyond my reach, so I found other ways of doing something worthwhile even when it involved going against the grain. Academics would have broadened my background as a musician. My hindsight advice to others is that school is a relatively short time in your life. If you can seriously apply yourself, use education to enhance your abilities, whatever they are.

Impromptu Jam Session

My mother isn't expecting company when the long blue bus pulls into the driveway. Fortunately for me, the scene becomes busy with musicians unloading me and a huge Hammond organ that they roll down the hill and into our spacious family room, not allowing time for questions from my mother. It would be totally out of character for her to have a problem with a lot of musicians and equipment entering our home unannounced, but I'm hoping to skip the part about me thumbin' a ride with a bus of prog rock musicians—two guitarists, a drummer, an organist and a singer. They just played a gig in Cleveland, and of course I invited them to a jam session at my house! The whole truth is that I hitch-hiked to Ann Arbor with my buddies to explore that college town's head shops and check out the record stores. I simply announce to Mom over the activity, "I brought some friends home. We're going to play some music."

When the group sets up and begins playing, I'm fascinated by how tight they are. They're all classically trained with music degrees, alternating instruments depending on the song. As they do a set of originals, I'm thinking, "Man, I envy these *cats." It's a great session that includes compositions in a style similar to Gentle Giant and King Crimson. These musicians are courageous, taking chances, traveling across the country and playing their own music. It's a quantum leap because there aren't too many unknown bands attempting this genre. They're actually getting bookings and making it work without big money behind them.

My mother's reaction to unexpected guests, this time people I don't even know, is classic Suzanne Lewis, warm and welcoming. There's never any doubt about my parents' hospitality toward all friends and musicians who enter our home, and I'm fully aware of how lucky I am to have the parents that I have. It also helps that our house has ample room for large sessions and a freight elevator that can accommodate larger pieces of equipment for full-blown ensembles. A Hammond organ? No sweat. This unplanned jam session in the mid-70s provides a wonderful experience for all, thanks to my mother and the warm, arms-open environment in our home.

Remorse

She's a sweet, sheltered Baptist girl. We attended the same elementary school, and now (1975) we're in high school together. Mega churches are the thing, and her parents attend one, wanting their daughter to live by norms and values consistent with those teachings. They're good people, but their lifestyle has resulted in a daughter who is naive. Even though she's an overtly obedient teenager, she's not really into the church scene and silently rejects it in favor of a more exciting inner voice—and mine.

We see each other for three years in spite of her mother and father being less than happy about their daughter hanging out with a musician, one with an unabashed secular perspective...to put it mildly. They want her to find a nice guy who attends church. I'm drawn to the beneath-the-surface unrest in this girl and introduce her to my world—a dark underworld compared to hers.

But who would think anything other than an innocent friendship is going on between us? In stark contrast to the life she lives, I spend evenings in nightclubs, smoking marijuana and drinking, unhindered by conservative principles and religious doctrine. I have no business being involved with her, but I don't care. I break all the rules and know better, pursuing my own agenda while her parents remain clueless about our activities.

One night after dinner with a couple of bottles of wine at an up-scale restaurant, we drop her off at home. She's giggling, weaving and tripping up the steps of the front porch. Just as she makes it to the top step, she falls face down near the front door. Giving me a look that lets me know I'm in deep shit, our driver (my dad) grunts loudly, "UGH!" as he gets out of the car. He carries her into the house, past her parents and to her room, their jaws dropping as he sheepishly bids them good evening. Needless to say, this ends of our innocent friendship. She wants to continue, but I call it quits.

Looking back now, I could have been more sensitive to her background. I was wild and cocky, believing I was all that and a bag of chips. We were a total mismatch, and I was a self-absorbed teenager. I embodied everything that her parents believed was wrong. I was glad she was finding her own way, but I should have been more respectful of our differences. In hindsight, parallel lines never cross. We were moving in the same direction but doomed to remain in separate lanes. The relationship was real but not really working. I hurt her, and I regret that. Years later, I apologized to her. She eventually married someone with a compatible lifestyle. I still feel guilt and remorse for bringing about the end of her innocence. To this day, I look back and realize that most of the relationships I've had with women didn't exist on common ground or even solid footing. Castles of sand wash into the sea.

CHAPTER THREE
Up & Down the Staircase

The title of this chapter reflects a recurring experience in New York City in the 1970s and 1980s from the perspective of a guy who isn't ambulatory. After you're carried down rickety stairs into a basement jazz or blues club, you have to make it back up the stairs at the end of the evening. Once you've been wheeled into the close quarters of a hotel service elevator, feeling like freight, you have to make the return trip to the floor where your room is—if the lift still works. Up and down the staircase, up and down between floors, driven by what's important, so important that you risk life and limb to get there and back. I've found religion several times on those creaky stairs and elevators. And, of course, there's the iconic staircase at the *Hotel Chelsea, an iron incline that has been tread by the famous and the infamous, one that my feet will never touch.

The sights and sounds of New York City are always a welcome break. Everybody is here—John Lennon, Frank Zappa, Richie Havens and some of the best jazz musicians in the world. I'm particularly drawn to *West Village with its cobblestone streets lined with old Federal-style townhouses, *Greenwich Village, and above all the music scene, small jazz clubs like *Village Vanguard and *Seventh Avenue South, places frequented by jazz and studio *cats. The renowned and infamous *Hotel Chelsea, domicile and haunt of masters and misfits of the arts, is my home away from home on many visits.

Grace

Thinking I've been fortunate to witness history being made during John Lennon's performance at the John Sinclair Freedom Rally in Crisler Arena at the University of Michigan on December 10, 1971, I'm certain it has been my one and only opportunity to see this living legend, but fate smiles again the following year.

Even though I don't have muscular dystrophy, Jerry Lewis invites me to the annual Muscular Dystrophy Telethon at the *Americana Hotel. When phone rings in my room, it's the producer, Woody Fraser. "John Lennon and Yoko Ono will be rehearsing downstairs real soon. Get yourself down there and you might get in." It's an easy jump into my wheelchair, and I make a mad dash for the elevator. I position myself near the entrance to the studio where the rehearsal will take place.

John appears slightly ahead of Yoko. He could easily hurry past me without acknowledging my presence. Many famous people would do just that, but without hesitation, John walks directly toward me and asks my name. "Dan Lewis. I'm a musician from Detroit." Yoko is approaching, and he calls to her, "Yoko, come and meet Dan." After a brief hello and without being asked, the two of them push my wheelchair through the studio door and directly up to the front. Before leaving me to take the stage, John asks, "Is everything cool?" I smile and nod as my internal voice is saying,

"How could everything not be cool, John?!" They rehearse and pre-record "Give Peace a Chance" with David Peel and Elephant's Memory. Even during this unforgettable, once-in-a-lifetime experience, I can't help being a die-hard music critic. David Peel and Elephant's Memory performing with John Lennon. Really?

To this day, I'm awestruck by the graciousness shown by John and Yoko when they readily acknowledged my presence and made sure I was given a place near the stage. Only three people were allowed in during that rehearsal.

Note about Yoko Ono: When she was receiving much criticism and being given little credit for her music and performances, I purchased her music, feeling she was a valid artist. I appreciated the unique way she used varying frequencies with her voice. It was impressive that she chose jazz saxophonist Ornette Coleman to play trumpet on a track titled "AOS" on her 1970 debut avant-garde studio album, *Yoko Ono/Plastic Ono Band*. I attended her multimedia art exhibit at the Cranbrook Museum in Bloomfield Hills, Michigan.

Music Vortex

I've had to trust others all my life and couldn't be in better hands tonight at *Seventh Avenue South in *Greenwich Village where the Brecker Brothers, Randy and Michael, have established this old-school jazz haven. Dave Liebman, George Mraz, Richie Beirach and John Abercrombie are unloading equipment when I arrive. They carry me down the narrow, rickety stairs into the renowned basement club.

Once inside, Dave greets me warmly. "Dan, thanks for coming out to hear us." The atmosphere is kindred and exhilarating at the same time...this place and these jazz icons. There's electricity in the air and a palpable soul in the floor and walls that must have seeped into the molecules of the place during melodic strains by music legends and on the breath of the jazz pioneers who performed and hung out here. Music wizardry happens in this room, and tonight it will take place with Dave Liebman on tenor and soprano sax, George Mraz on bass, Peter Donald on drums, John Abercrombie on guitar and Richie Beirach on piano and electronic synthesizer.

> **Art is constant tension and release.**
> **That is where artists live, between the two,**
> **or at times, submerged in either.**
>
> *Dave Liebman*

The performance—essence of improv, true mastery, mesmerizing, flawless, weaving and cascading in one voice. As endorphins are released, I'm transformed. I'm here in the Promised Land, drawn in soul to soul. Never have I heard musicians travel so well together with parallel and intersecting parts and so much trust in each other. I've never experienced anything like it before or since.

I'm in awe of Dave. He's a supreme *cat with international reach who channels the spirit of Coltrane. He chats with me after the performance, and I feel an undeniable chemistry with this extraordinary human being. So begins a lifelong friendship on this night in 1980.

Night Brawlers

The iconic staircase. I wish I could climb those steps just because they're here in the *Hotel Chelsea and have been tread by so many legendary artists and musicians. Larry Fratangelo, Dan Oestrike and I have taken a room here, mostly for the Chelsea's ambiance, while we're in New York City to help a friend move. If it can be believed that a physical space absorbs the energies of those who occupy it, this hotel has. The *prana* of talented and tortured souls lingers in the hallways and rooms. It's also the real-time haunt of artists who, in spite of their fame, exist on the periphery of society, hardly the type to stay at a bland, run-of-the-mill Hyatt or Radisson.

Snow is piling up in drifts outside, so we settle in with a bottle and go to bed feeling mellow, but our sleep will be punctuated—with exclamation points. A night-long war of agony and passion in the room across the hall begins with loud yelling and crying, escalating with shrieks and crashing background noises. The commotion continues for quite a while, and we're thinking they'll either kill each other or fall into a drug- or alcohol-induced coma. In either case, we'll get some sleep. Not. It continues well beyond what most impaired brawlers would have the capacity to endure. I'm lying here knowing it would be futile to call the front desk—always a freak show here.

Before long, the action overflows into our room when a man walks in, apparently oblivious to any occupants here, yelling over his shoulder in the direction of the room across the hall. We tell him to get out, and he does. Neither Larry nor Dan O. gets out of bed to secure the door because it seems to have a broken lock. Over the next few hours, we catch short naps during periods of truce only to be awakened by repeated bouts of crashing, screaming and wailing until finally I exclaim, "Damn! This has to stop sometime tonight!" In classic Fratangelo fashion, Larry grumbles in the dark, "Who gives a fuck? Shut up and go to sleep. If we get killed, we get killed."

After a while, there's a prolonged silence. Just as I'm drifting off to sleep, the door opens and the man enters our room again as if it's his own, his image visible in the faint glow of streetlights through a window. He sits down on the far end of the sofa and sighs as if he's relieved to be in a safe zone. A woman soon joins him on the couch, and there's just enough light to see that both of them are bruised and bleeding. He's half reclining, and she props her bare feet on the coffee table, very cozy. They're fully aware that we're present because they nonchalantly ask us for a drink as if they're guests at a cocktail party. Never mind that they don't know us and we're in bed for the night. Again, neither Larry nor Dan gets up, probably the smartest response. The interlopers remain in our room for a prolonged period of time during which there are heated episodes of disjointed, circular dialogue interspersed with long moments of brooding and sighing. Then they leave, slamming the door behind them. I'm thinking that if we try to somehow block the door after their lengthy visit, they might feel like they've been evicted. They might even kick it in. During the remainder of the night, their entrance-and-exit routine is repeated a couple more times. Considering where we are, Larry, Dan and I just stay put, hoping they'll kill each other before their aggression turns on us. In the morning, the door to our room is ajar, and there's silence behind the door of the room across the hall. They're gone, comatose or dead.

I've since wondered if the night brawlers were even real. Perhaps they were restless spirits trapped in Chelsea Time.

Jaco

Dan Oestrike and I make the acquaintance of bass guitarist Jaco Pastorius in the bathroom at an Ann Arbor, Michigan music venue where he's performing with his jazz fusion band, Word of Mouth. He's on tour to promote an album by the same name, his second solo project. He's not shy or embarrassed about telling us that he's unhappy with his guys, ironically because they're too high, telling us he needs them to stay on their game. We talk for a bit before he goes on stage, and he makes sure we're seated in the front row.

Later the same year (1981), a Detroit drummer friend and I are at *Sweet Basil, a jazz club in *Greenwich Village, New York City when Jaco walks in. We're here for a performance by the Gil Evans Orchestra. When Jaco sees me, he says, "I remember you. Your name is Dan. Good to see you again." I tell him that I dig what he's been writing, compositions with a non-traditional big band sound. This is music to Jaco's ears because he's an insecure artist with a big ego.

Between sets we go out on the street where Gil's band members are sitting on the hood of a Chevy Impala with their legs dangling. Jaco appears outside. His manic state is providing quite a sideshow, especially for the student from Paris who's here with him. Jaco yells into the air, "I'm the greatest bass player in the world!" as chuckles are heard from Gil's musicians. I'm thinking how such an unhumble exclamation by this bipolar genius, lightning in a bottle, is probably true. Then he proclaims, "I own *SoHo!" and insists on showing my friend and me around. He leads us to a few more bars and clubs, all three of us drunk and high. Even in our euphoric state, Jaco and I talk about the physical endurance required for a percussionist. Amazingly, he has the presence of mind to advise me on the importance of physical exercise to a percussionist's upper body strength, showing genuine caring and kindness.

Jaco doesn't want my companion's continued presence but at the same time is hoping to get more of his cocaine. He pushes my wheelchair fast ahead, hoping to put some distance between us and my sidekick as he bends down and talks into my ear, "Let's go shoot some hoop!" He wheels me through *SoHo toward a park, losing patience with my feet because they're dragging the pavement. "Lift your feet! We've gotta pick up the pace and get into a rhythm!" My friend catches up with us at the park where Jaco, nimble and athletic, is coaching me on how to shoot baskets from my chair. When we part later, Jaco says he'll come to our hotel tomorrow, adding, "If I'm not there, I'll be doin' somethin' else." At this moment, I know we won't see him tomorrow.

I'm going to blame alcohol and cocaine for the remainder of the evening. My buddy and I return to the hotel where there's a very attractive woman standing on the sidewalk. She doesn't appear to be lost, checking into the hotel or waiting for a taxi. After saying hello and a making a visual sweep of the surrounding area, she tells me, "You're handsome" and asks, "Would you like to spend some time with me?" Recognizing what's being implied, my buddy disappears. Instead of declining her offer or going directly up to my room with her, I suggest that we go to the nearby *Hotel Chelsea for coffee. I've always enjoyed exploring off the main road, and I find the lives of people who live outside the mainstream fascinating. We talk for a long time about minds, hearts and life. For me, sex is a side dish, so it isn't until after coffee and a couple of drinks that we go to my room.

While I'm upstairs with the lady, my friend goes outside to smoke and gets rolled by some thugs who take his money, what's left of the coke, and for whatever reason, his glasses. I go down to the lobby later, but my friend isn't there. I find him bewildered, broke and blind as a bat on the front steps of the hotel. Assuming that someone whose cocaine they've stolen won't call the police, the thieves are hanging out in the lobby, having drinks. I decide to approach them, wagering that they won't attack a guy in a wheelchair in plain sight in the lobby of a hotel. "You've taken all my friend's money and his glasses. He can't see, and we have to get through the rest of the week in the city." I don't mention the cocaine. They look at each other, one of them putting a hand over his heart and tilting his head as he feigns pity for us, and they hand me the glasses.

What a night! New York City has a way of kicking your ass, a real adult dose, but you love it so much that you can't wait to return.

Note regarding Jaco Pastorius: It was apparent in 1981 that he was on a collision course with life. He eventually developed a pattern of provoking bar fights and then allowing himself to be beaten up. On September 11, 1987, he was refused entrance at the Midnight Bottle Club in Wilton Manors, Florida and became involved in a confrontation with the bar manager who was a martial arts expert. Jaco sustained multiple injuries and lapsed into a coma. He was removed from life support on September 21. As far as I'm concerned, Jaco was one of the pioneers of electric bass as a front melodic instrument in jazz, a true innovator and frontrunner within the genre. We'll never see the likes of him again.

CHAPTER FOUR
Elusive Expectations

A dream all by itself can be a setup for disappointment and disillusionment. Thinking that fame in the music business is tied to wealth or even financial well-being is a fantasy. The truth is that most rock stars aren't rich. Too many artists and bands believe their immediate goal should be getting signed by a record label. This short-sightedness sets the stage for disappointment. There's no consistent set of practices across the music industrial complex. Different companies use different playbooks, but their focus, priorities and resources are driven by the dollar, not by considerations for the welfare of the artist except to the extent that the artist's image and sound promote sales. Listeners love a big hit splash, unaware of artistic and financial compromises that have been made by the artist.

Many greats perform on the periphery of national and international landscapes, every bit as talented as the famous artists they accompany and support, backing them up on tour and in recording studios. This observation was made by Andy Newmark in a 2014 Rocky and the Natives (English country rock band) radio interview when he said, "A lot of great talent won't ever rise to the top." Todd Rundgren said the dream goes on forever. I believe dedicated musicians keep on doing what they do for the love of the music.

> I never waited for something to happen—I just went out
> and did it. I didn't wait for acclaim or affirmation or anything like that.
> I always kept myself busy and wrote music. Some people think
> that success only comes through the front door, so they're waiting
> at that door. Truth is, sometimes it comes in the back door...
> Just keep busy and do what you're meant to do.
> If you do that, it'll all come together.
>
> *Todd Rundgren*
> *Founder and President, *Spirit of Harmony Foundation*
> *Guitar World, June 2015*

Broad acclaim is often an outcome of networking with those who might open doors. However one defines success, it usually doesn't happen because someone discovers you, and it sure doesn't come knocking on your door. Many gifted musicians don't know how to market themselves or their product if that word should even be used in reference to art. Others find the business end of music distasteful, or it involves skills they don't possess or can't afford to pay for. Basic administrative coordination and at least enough business acumen to understand the language and implications of a contract are survival necessities. Musicians must be able to read, interpret and grasp the implications of a contract.

Success has not yet arrived when an artist gets "signed." Some artists are shelved by a record label, held hostage by an exclusivity clause that won't allow them to pursue other opportunities and kept in a corporate pocket just in case another signed artist doesn't generate a profit. Others are passed over like Eva Cassidy, a singer with a heavenly voice, when *Blue Note promoted Norah Jones instead. I believe they did it because Norah was younger and therefore more visually marketable. Another reality that artists need to be aware of is that contracts can require them to pay back costs to the company. Doing so can take years beyond the duration of an artist's time in the spotlight. There have also been instances of companies retaining the rights to music that was written by the songwriter or composer. For these reasons and more, artists have long considered the practices of record companies to be predatory.

And there's the industry's closed doors and inbreeding. When Josh Sulfaro was taking a class on music for film and television at UCLA, the panel of industry insiders was less than encouraging. Asked by one of the attendees about the process to get music placed, the answer was, "My response to inquiries is that I'm not interested because I don't know you." Adding to the brutal message, another industry muckety-muck told the class, "We don't care how good your music is. If it doesn't come to us through someone we know, we won't consider it." When asked why these barriers exist, the response was that producers don't know what they're listening to and can't judge whether it's good and also that they won't consider an unknown who might be unreliable. The message: You'll have to suck up to an insider or garner consideration under the wing of someone who's already known in the industry. After years of writing, recording and doing live performances in greater Detroit followed by four years in Los Angeles and three years in Nashville, Josh concluded that he was wasting time and sold catalogs of his compositions, some worthy of film soundtracks, to a music publisher/library. His music has found placement in Europe, Australia, Canada and Mexico.

I had a similar experience at a drum clinic in Chicago with successful, well known instructors (Steve Gadd, Ralph MacDonald). On the subject of music producers, attendees were truthfully told, "There are too many people in L.A. and New York City, so they only call the guys they know." In other words, "You guys might as well forget it because the field is saturated." I remember calling the instructors out on the discouraging impact of the statements. To be fair, they added that if one wants to hang in there and push, there's a chance of breaking through—if you relocate to where the industry is. That part of their message was a good one, and I've observed the truth in it when great musicians have remained in Detroit instead of moving to a music industry hub. I'm torn between thinking students deserve to be told the realities and believing mentors shouldn't knock the wind out of the sails of those who are striving.

It's a pity and a tragedy that the public at large only becomes aware of musicians and music that are allowed entry into the industry's inner sanctum. This is the reason some of the greatest musicians and some of the best music ever written will never be heard. Unfortunately, the music business is mostly a land of broken dreams. Los Angeles, Renaissance City, should rightly be called Hollywouldn't because it's a place where insect spray is used on butterflies.

The same has been true of Nashville where, with some exceptions, well known artists have gained entry into country music through industry insiders. Tune in and listen to the songs. Then judge whether or not new country sounds are predominantly alike. The good news is that there are diverse genres coming out of Nashville. It's no longer just a country music mecca and finally resembles its name, Music City USA, thanks to newer residents who have brought more varieties of music including the New Americana sound. There are artists like Neko Case, Sam Bush and Robben Ford as well as others including Steve Winwood and Jack White who have either moved their residence or operations to Nashville. It's a place where there are live performances seven nights per week, providing the truly gifted musicians with venues for showcasing their performance and songwriting abilities. Younger *cats are no longer confined to a box, but Nashville's expanded reach is also creating another over-saturated music industry hub. Fortunately, the internet has also given artists independence as well as other avenues for their music.

> **Dream the dream until it clings to your life like skin.**
> **Expand this horizon. It's the season. Lift the gate.**
> *From "Dream the Dream"*
> *in Memoirs de Nocturne: An Anthology*
> *Abe Sulfaro (1970-2014), Detroit musician, author and poet*

During a 1980 visit with Bernard Purdie at his Harlem apartment to discuss a potential performance at Ford Auditorium in Detroit that ultimately didn't work out because of money, I received some solid advice from the legendary drummer. Our conversation had arrived at the hard realities of the music business and how artists struggle to break through barriers. In regard to pursuing dreams that run up against the statement "It's just the way things are," Bernard advised me to disregard that crap. "Bust down doors to get what you're after." With a defiant look, he spouted, "Bullshit on needing connections. There's another way. Push your own expectations and believe in yourself. If you're clear about what you're going for, trust yourself and stay determined. You can do anything. Determination and ego are how I developed the Purdie Shuffle and signature beats. I trusted myself while I was doing it." Bernard intuitively knew I was in need, searching. As I was leaving, he added, "And one more thing. Always stay on your game."

Over the years, I stayed at Bernard's place in Harlem when I was in New York City, and he stayed at my house when he was playing in Detroit. To this day, I'm grateful that he coached me up. Music industry barricades bring out defiance in me, push me into Fuck You Territory, and I lace up my kick-down-the-door boots. Determination will get you everywhere. I'll maintain an awareness of prevailing conditions but also hold onto my dreams and take the disappointments as they come. The keys are right there in your pocket...where you keep them.

Expectations and reality are managed by a genius, a term that gets thrown around a lot. To me, a genius is an artist who finds a way to be self-contained in order to pursue a vision on his or her own terms. Frank Zappa wanted to write classical music and used rock 'n roll as a commercial vehicle toward that end. He paved his own detour around the agenda and methods of the recording industry. The careers of Zappa, Pat Metheny, Herbie Hancock and Chick Corea expose a functional imbalance in their management of reality in pursuit of expectations and visions. They're driven, laser-focused and indefatigable. Being involved in their pursuits means you either go with their vision or get left in the dust. They have no time for anyone else's input if it doesn't fit or advance their visions, resulting in others having to accept subjugation of personal ideas and artistic preferences. The quests of these geniuses take no breaks or vacations.

Sometimes expectations aren't aligned with reality or they clash outright. Such is the case with my tendency to want aging idols to keep doing what they've always done, even when they need to slow down and breathe. I expect them to be on stage, performing and touring. No mercy! I rage against the expectation that you retire when you reach a certain age and enter your "Golden Years," consensus reality jive used to sell retirement plans. Dan Rather's interviews with Merle Haggard and Neil Young touch on the topic of retirement. Each of them is asked, "Why do you keep on?" Neil responds to Rather, himself a man continuing to work well into his senior years, with, "What are you doin'? You're doing what you love to do." Haggard answers Rather, "I'm scared of the loneliness." He also says family members are mere acquaintances compared to fans who love him for the performance and adds, "I think it keeps you alive." Van Morrison has said he'll get sick if he doesn't sing. Elvin Jones told me, "Once a musician, always a musician." I guess that's where I'm coming from. Your life's passion is who you are; it doesn't leave you, and you don't just stop.

The basic fault in my selfish notion is that slowing down or retiring has to be considered from the perspective of each artist. They deserve to scale it on their own terms, decelerating or retreating entirely if that's what they want to do, as they continue to create or play for personal pleasure. An artist might even choose to become completely dormant for myriad reasons.

One of the advantages of yesteryear (late 1960s to early 1990s) was that record companies got radio time for potential hits, building a fan base for artists. In those days, a successful artist might be signed for 25 years and allowed to grow within the label like Bob Dylan with Columbia Records. When opportunities present themselves nowadays and doors open, few musicians enjoy sustained success within the mainstream market. The industry has been changed by technology and a culture that lives from moment to moment on hit 'n run sound bites. You must build your own fan base through online sites where fans click on "Like" and then demonstrate substantial sales. If you've made money for a company, you must do the same again and again and again or you're thrown overboard. You have little creative control, initially because you need to sound like a proven product, an artist or group that makes money for the company, and later because of the need to crank out hits like you're on a production line, no time for development of artistry and certainly nothing unique. Frank Zappa (1940-1993) spoke of this when he observed that the American focus is on an instant bottom line and that culturally, we're okay with mediocrity (2016 documentary *Eat That Question: Frank Zappa in His Own Words*).

Jazz has always been different from rock and pop. It's more about the creative endeavor. If a jazz artist gets signed, contract duration is short because fewer units are expected to be sold, and there's a presumption that the product will continue to breathe on its own. Jazz musicians can make a living doing live performances. If they're well known enough to continue, they can maintain a revenue stream, but they don't plan on making a lot of money. Rock is becoming more like jazz in terms of earning potential, and new country is becoming more like pop in terms of its commerciality, recurring sound templates and the flash-in-the-pan nature of its tunes and artists. One of the things that bothers me most about the current state of music is that streamed and downloaded songs lack the ambiance, enchantment and excitement that live in the sound, feel and smell of vinyl.

There is hope. Corporate interests in music aren't as powerful as they once were because artists are using the internet to build their own market, but it's a double-edged sword. On the one hand, it has given artists a route to independence, but on the other hand, the internet has hurt artists by giving listeners access to cheap and free downloads of music. You can be in charge of your own business which is a good thing, but you'd better know the business. Do you have a written business plan? Do you have a marketing plan and a production/distribution plan in the event of high volume demand? The greatest opportunity right now is for singer-songwriters, but no artist has the luxury of just being the artist. In addition to providing downloads, you must be able to perform live for videos and streaming, and much time must be invested in online outreach.

I try to grasp what's goin' down in real time with an awareness that situations and events are filtered through my own expectations, hopes and dreams...visions that can seduce and elude me. As observed by jazz pianist/composer/arranger Horace Silver (1928-2014) in the song "Cause and Effect," I'm the winner and the loser. Each thought, word and deed plant a seed that I may have to reap eventually. Silver's lyrics speak to me like the Buddhist belief in intention and deliberate deeds, both spoken and thought of, that lead to future consequences. I need to live where good things stick to the wall. If I don't trust the packaged program, I reject it and forge ahead on my own terms. I've learned to stick around for the moment and tune in to what it's layin' down because it might not come around again.

Risk and Reward

Dan Lewis, producer-promoter. I decide to try the role in 1987 because all things are connected. The more abilities you develop, the greater your overall synergy. Musicians who include Joe LoDuca and Ralph Towner are doing events in Recital Hall at the Detroit Institute of Arts, so I set up a composer-performer event: Dave Liebman and Richie Beirach at the Detroit Institute of Arts. They've been recording as a saxophone-piano duo. It's important music, culturally elevating, and it's getting lots of traction. They do a suite of their originals with some Coltrane classics on a Sunday evening. Turnout is so-so, but those who attend dig it.

Here's what I learn about the producer-promoter role. Fronting money is high risk. If radio stations provide free air time for advertising, as WDET-FM public radio did for our event, it's not really free. They expect you to "comp" a number of tickets, thereby reducing profit. I am, however, grateful to Judy Adams, Program Director at WDET, for providing the promo spots. In the end, the event is a net monetary loss, but it puts great music out in front of the public, so it's not a total bust. Matt Michaels, a musician and educator, arranges for Dave and Richie, educators themselves, to do a couple of clinics at Wayne State University while they're in town.

*Dan Lewis & Friends

It takes four years to reach a decision to form a big band of my own, a group that performs arrangements in the style of the

James Last Orchestra and Tower of Power and also inspired by Blood, Sweat & Tears and Todd Rundgren's band and his album *Nearly Human*. I want to do something with my own jazz spin on it, not to mention that the R&B/soul genre has yet to be fully explored, so I consider all the possibilities including the use of *contrafact for dynamic effect and "wow" factor. My vision includes musicians from various genres who can reach beyond the usual and make our sound unique. When people leave a performance, they should feel that they've heard something special.

Overall, I achieve my vision even though we're not always as well rehearsed as we might be due to the number of musicians—11 to 18 of them (listed by name in Index). The logistics and space required for practice sessions are challenging. I learn that it takes time to write charts, making sure all the parts are included, and that everything depends on what's on the page. Once the tune is there, you can have fun with improvisation by stretching the solo sections. When doing funky R&B, the horns must be in unison.

Our regional reach from 1990 to 2002 is owed to a number of people including Shelly Baghdadi and Maureen Daley, booking agents and firebrands for *Dan Lewis & Friends; Huel Perkins, Fox 2 TV news personality; and musician/arranger/composer/promoter, Alexander Zonjic. I sometimes front the money because venues can't afford to pay such a large group. You must bring your own following. Club owners expect it, and they don't necessarily promote an event. Because of these realities, not to mention my quest for BIG which is cost-prohibitive, *Dan Lewis and Friends doesn't book nearly as many performances as I've hoped for. As it turns out, my vision produces the desired effect with very special artists who remain to this day in my orbit of friends.

I've learned that having a vision isn't enough, especially if it's a lofty vision. Business acumen and a written business plan are indispensable. Viability comes down to how you proceed within the plan. Along with a generous consideration of reality, the plan should include goals, specific milestones and how far you expect to take the vision. No judgment here about musicians who don't have built-in business skills. After all, business education has been a relatively late addition to the curricula at music schools, so having a business resource with know-how can make or break the plan's success.

After All (song by Al Jarreau)

I meet Al Jarreau in 1990 through Maureen Daley, booking agent for *Dan Lewis & Friends, at *Metro Music Café during the Walk of Fame event in Royal Oak. We hit it off right away, but I'm a lousy fan, not into celebrity and not after an autograph. Al quickly recognizes that it's totally about the music for me. He knows I respect his talent and artistry, and beyond that, I want to know him as a person. I write to Al and go to his performances all over the country. We get to know each other well and have an ongoing friendship until his death in 2017.

Al advises me on things like music demos, exercise and health, the topic depending on his mood. Sometimes he asks for my input on what he should record. Coming from the perspective of a genre stickler, I don't hesitate to tell him that I think he's gone commercial. Al has the ability to do something by Lionel Hampton and then turn around and do the theme song for the TV series *Moonlighting*. I feel he's at his best as a traditional jazz *cat and to a lesser degree when he does smooth jazz for the money. He calls me a purist. At one point, he tells me, "Why should I even tell you what I'm thinking about recording? You aren't gonna buy it anyway." Man, he's got my number. Ironically for someone who strives to make it real, I wear blinders when it comes to genre and economics.

Al Jarreau left, Dan Lewis right.
Fox Theater, Detroit, 1990

When I love an artist's work, I deep-dive. At times, I'm a painstaking listener to music, not for enjoyment but as if dissecting a specimen. I listen for time signatures, chord structures, where the melody travels, the bass lines, the bridge and the arrangement, mentally processing the parts of the composition and how they come together in unified wholeness. When I'm driven by a desire to perform, I crawl inside a piece hundreds of times. While others are enjoying the music, my dispassionate ass is analyzing it to exhaustion. This is why I'm confident that I can do Al Jarreau's music justice and believe I belong in his tour band as a percussionist. I learn Al's music over twenty years, listening to recordings of him with percussionists Lenny Castro and Paulinho Da Costa. I'm aware that these famous *cats aren't always on Al's tours because of the expense. It's not that I think I'm as good as they are, but I've listened to them so many times that their licks are recorded in my gray matter and hardwired in my hands. I know everything about the tunes—their character, nature, rhythms, changes. This knowing can be trusted, and I'm cocky enough to be sure that I can enhance Al's live performances, so I propose that I become his percussionist for tours. I offer to provide my own caregiver on the road, and I'm persistent. I'll take excellent care of Al's music, his children. Speaking in lingo familiar to him, I tell him emphatically, "I'm serious, mother fucker! I can help make your music better than I found it."

All my ego needs is a good rhythm section.
Miles Davis

In the end, I'm not hired for Al's tours based on the reservations of those who surround and advise him. Life on the road is tough, and it's much easier to climb on and off planes, buses and stages with someone who's not in a wheelchair. But I don't disappear, definitely not me. If a rock hits me in the head and I go down in the street, it ain't over until someone confirms, "Dan is dead." I want to perform with Al, but the naysayers around him are always interfering. They wonder why he would want to incur the extra expense or invest the effort involved with a handicapped band member. I let them know that I'm willing to pay for my own caregiver, but I don't think they really get that or even care to. It's much easier to hire another *cat. Al is conflicted and doesn't know what to do with me. In pursuit of becoming a member of his tour band, I record demos and give them to him. He says, "Man, I love these," but he seems unable to commit due to counter-pressures.

Backstage with George Benson at Pine Knob, Al tells those present, "I've known Dan longer than any of you *cats. This guy belongs to me!" He listens to *Dan Lewis & Friends recordings and gives me his opinion. Al looks lovingly inside my head where an elusive butterfly named Perfection is constantly fluttering about. He really listens...beyond my recordings and my purist opinions about music. He encourages me and relates to me as a brother. He understands that because of my handicap, I need everything that I do to be a cut above, no mediocrity. But he also reminds me that I tend to allow a quest for perfection to get in the way.

Al Ayoub pushes my wheelchair downhill at the Trenton (Michigan) Smooth Jazz Festival, through security and throngs of people to the stage near the river. The venue is familiar. *Dan Lewis & Friends has performed here several times, and this year it's being hosted by a friend, Alexander Zonjic.

Al Jarreau spots me immediately as he's stepping off the golf cart that transports performers to the stage. He has changed, frailer than the last time I saw him and slightly bent over. He greets me with a warm embrace, eager to tell me what he's been up to. As usual, he begins with crisp, clear *scat (vocal percussion), this time in Guaguancó-like rhythm followed by, "Dan, Jay Graydon called. We're going to try to make some hits again." There's a pause and I nod, acknowledging the update. He adds, "You look well. Do you need anything?" I'm sensing something. Al's essence is as vibrant as ever, but his body is weak.

As we talk again after his performance, it's even more apparent that he's struggling physically. Before we part, he bends down to my level and kisses me on the lips. "Don't worry, man. The album will be out next year. I'll see you then." The love is palpable. At this moment, I know I'll never see him again, not in this lifetime. Ultimately, the recording with Graydon never takes place. There's a lump in my throat, an inner voice wailing, "Yes, Al, I'll see you somewhere."

My 27-year friendship with Al Jarreau was one of love and understanding until his death in 2017. I didn't get to tour with you this time around, Al, but someday...when I shed this body.

Parallel Realities (album by Jack DeJohnette)

Drummer-pianist-composer-arranger Jack DeJohnette is getting ready to take the stage with Herbie Hancock, Pat Metheny and Dave Holland at Meadow Brook Theatre (Rochester, Michigan) during their 1991 tour to promote Jack's album *Parallel Realities*. We're having dinner backstage, and Jack and I get into a conversation about creating melodies on drums. Masters know there's a lot more to drums than keeping time. I tell him, "When I listen to you, I'm totally absorbed by the sounds you create." He knows how sincerely interested I am and replies that playing piano has helped with that. It makes sense. I wish I'd studied piano because it opens up harmonic concepts.

Jack, Dave and I talk about how European influence has broadened the jazz landscape and made it accessible to a larger audience. The world at large has done so much to advance American music, jazz in particular. It's more widely enjoyed in

Europe than in the U.S. This is why so many jazz musicians work in Europe and even reside there.

Then Jack asks, "How would you like to be engulfed in sound tonight?" Before I can answer, he adds, "You're going on stage with me. I'll wheel you out and you'll sit next to me and the drums." Aside from thinking I'll be a fifth wheel on stage, I'm excited to be included by a jazz virtuoso like Jack DeJohnette! I ask him, "Are you sure, Jack?" As he wheels me out on stage, a member of the Meadow Brook management staff tells him, "You can't do that. He's not in the group." Jack turns to him and asks, "Whose name is on the marquee?" End of discussion. It's a stellar concert, one of the best live performances I've ever experienced, and I have the best seat in the house.

(L to R) English jazz double bassist Dave Holland,
Dan Lewis, American jazz drummer and pianist Jack DeJohnette.
Meadow Brook Theatre, Rochester, Michigan, 1991.
Tour to promote Jack's album *Parallel Realities*
with jazz guitarist Pat Metheny and pianist Herbie Hancock

Jack was one of the first to endorse the electronic wave drum. Because of him, I purchased one. It gave me another option, a percussive orchestra in one little instrument.

Chemistry

"The chord voicings in this arrangement should be clear." This statement during a collaborative endeavor results in two options. The person on the receiving end of it can either spend time and energy pushing back by selling and convincing or go with the flow as a project partner pleaser. In most instances, collaboration is a pursuit entered into with the best intentions and hope for a good outcome. You start out thinking that if you have quality ingredients, you'll make a great meal. What often happens, however, is that one partner's preferences and vision dominate the project. This has been my experience, and I'm not saying this as the underdog. I've been on offense and on defense. Sometimes there are differences in abilities to write music charts that can be read and understood by others. Even more challenging are differences in interpretation. What is being heard by one person can be at odds with what the other person hears.

Collaboration. The word is thrown around when referring to an activity, but true collaboration is an elusive state of being. When it happens, it's unforeseen, like love at first sight, and has consequential results. Can two hang gliders hold hands? Suppose they don't even have to hold hands, each one of them instinctively knowing where they're headed together? In this sense, is hang gliding simply an activity or is it an entwined state of being? Steely Dan's Donald Fagen and Walter Becker were writing partners who were so in synch with each other that they could finish each other's sentences. No energy was wasted on opposing perspectives, differing interpretations or second-guessing. This kind of chemistry, based on mutual respect and trust, guides the creation of music.

Butterfly Nets

Happiness, another word that's used as if it's something every-one hopes to attain as a state of being. In reality it's an elusive emotion that visits in fleeting moments. My thoughts are similar to two other Detroit musicians, Jack White in an interview with Dan Rather and Abe Sulfaro in his novel *The Antiheroes: Treatise of a Lost Soul.* Both artists refer to the "pursuit" of happiness, neither of them believing it's a steady state to be arrived at like enlightenment or self-actualization. People do find fulfillment and some measure of contentment, but like Jack and Abe, I don't believe happiness is possible as a constant in one's existence, not during this earthbound life. Happiness doesn't reside here, but I do enjoy brief visits by its siblings, joy and enchantment, as alluded to by jazz saxophonist/flutist/philosopher Rahsaan Roland Kirk: "Bright moments, bright moments, right now."

Moments of elation and ecstasy, most of them related to music, enrich my life. I try to savor them. I keep quiet and soak them in...if allowed. This is why I sometimes go to performances by myself. People talk too much instead of focusing their audio on the music. They kill the buzz by describing and analyzing quality or impact, how rippin' cool a piece of music is, who wrote it, the chord progressions, while you're trying to enjoy it! Poorly timed chatter interrupts moments of awe and wonder.

CHAPTER FIVE
Hallowed Ground, Scorched Earth

An Evening with The Byrds

The Byrds are in Detroit to promote their 1965 album *Turn! Turn! Turn!* Miles Davis and The Byrds share the same manager, and Miles has referred to them as American Beatles. Having been a Byrds fan since their song "Mr. Tambourine Man," I'm ecstatic about the opportunity to hang out with them over dinner at the Lamplighter in Lincoln Park. This connection is possible through a family acquaintance who is a music promoter and manager for The Mastertones, currently notable due to a performance with the Rolling Stones at Cobo Hall.

I'm well versed in jazz, blues and progressive music and artists. We talk about John Coltrane, Miles Davis, Odetta, The Clancy Brothers, Pete Seeger and Bob Dylan. I see their looks of amazement that a kid my age (seven years old) knows about Sonny Boy Williamson and Lightnin' Hopkins. David Crosby recounts the influence Coltrane has had on his own music, citing the inspiration for "Eight Miles High." I've been taking drum lessons (trap drums) and tell the drummer, Michael Clarke, that I'm motivated to play like him and Charlie Watts. The evening is exciting for me and I hope enjoyable for them.

Years later, I discover that The Wrecking Crew, revered L.A. studio musicians, played on the first Byrds album. In the 1960s, Top 40 radio was king, so the record labels kept it quiet when studio musicians were used because they were selling the image of the band. Studio musicians were used to get an arrangement recorded as near perfect as possible, not only to maximize the sale of 45s but also because 45s sold albums. The market was driven by singles, but I tended to purchase albums because I wanted to know as much as possible about the music and the artists. To this day, I still do.

Stage Doors

I begin going to Detroit nightclubs and music venues in the late 1960s and continue to be a fixture at those places through the early 1980s. Music is uncomplicated. It's close to the audience, intimate. You see artists in their natural habitats: Elmwood Casino in Windsor, Ontario (just across the river from Detroit), the *Roostertail, *Dummy George's, *Watts Club Mozambique, *The 20 Grand, *The Palladium, *Eastown Theatre, *Bert's Marketplace, *Strata Concert Gallery, *Cobb's Corner, *Cinderella Ballroom, *Baker's Keyboard Lounge and the *Grande Ballroom, a.k.a. Detroit's Rock 'n Roll Palace. I'm a cockroach that keeps getting into the house through a crack in the wall, in this case the back doors. The greats play in these places: Ray Charles, Earl Grant, Nancy Wilson, Barbara McNair, Spyder Turner, Major Lance, Wilbur Harrison, Martha Reeves, Marvin Gaye and Blood Sweat & Tears.

I meet Russ Gibb, *Grande Ballroom operator who is a DJ and rock promoter, at a Canned Heat concert at the Masonic Temple and begin calling WKNR-FM while Russ is hosting on-the-air panel discussions. Impressed with my knowledge of blues and its legends such as Ma Rainey, Bessie Smith, Big Mama Thornton and Detroiter Sippie Wallace, Russ asks, "Are you for real?" After that, I'm often on the air with him, and sometimes I go to the station. Over the years, Russ not only gives me easy entry into the *Grande but also takes me to parties and events where I can interact with music greats including Jeff Beck and Rod Stewart.

Many years later in 2012, I'm in the audience at *The Fillmore during an on-stage panel discussion. The panel consists of notables who include MC5 co-founder Wayne Kramer and record producer Jack Douglas. The topic is the premiere of the movie *Louder than Love: The Grande Ballroom Story*. I take the microphone from the audience to add history and context and also to acknowledge Russ Gibb for allowing me to experience the Grande at such a young age. Wayne Kramer adds, "Unlike the filmmakers, Dan has actually been to the Grande."

Thanks to all the stage doors and the music inside them during the early years, I become focused like a laser beam. I enter and the magic begins. Theater and club owners allow me to sit in the wings of the stage, and I'm given full access to performers. The entrance to *Eastown Theatre is welcoming, my door to another world. It's here that I meet Van Morrison, Leslie West, the Allman Brothers and Rod Stewart when he's performing with Jeff Beck. It doesn't take these *cats more than a few minutes to know I'm a serious music devotee. When Rod comes to town, even after moving on to the band Faces, he checks in to see how I'm doing and picks me up to go to the shows at the *Eastown or leaves a pass for me at the door. But my heaven creates more frustration in my life. Out with Rod Stewart one night and, *ugh*, back in school the next day.

A favorite spot is *Baker's Keyboard Lounge on Livernois where live jazz has been played since 1934. It's here that I experience performances by Jimmy Smith, Wes Montgomery and Larry Young. Mr. (Clarence) Baker lets me in the back door, knowing I'm too young to be inside. I meet Coltrane's drummer, Elvin Jones, here in the '70s and develop a 12-year friendship with him and his wife, composer-arranger Keiko Jones. During Elvin's gigs at Baker's into the mid-1980s, Elvin and Keiko pick me up at my home on Grosse Ile, and after the performances they drive me back. Mom makes breakfast for us, and Elvin listens to recordings with me. When he's doing a week-long engagement at Baker's, he asks if I'd like him to pick me up the next day. I decline his gracious offer when it's for repeat trips during one week because it's 30 miles one way.

Tracks

Detroit provides great experiences in sound reinforcement. Leslie West (1945-2020) and Rod Stewart sometimes pick me up hours before their performances and take me to rehearsals and sound checks where I get to observe, listen and talk to the sound engineers. During two- and three-night engagements, I observe improvement night after night, all the nuances dialed in. My ears are being prepped.

There's no question that I prefer doing live performances, but I also enjoy the recording studio and owe so much to the experience gained during the mid-1970s through the 1990s. George

Clinton embraces all creative possibilities in order to get "inside the funk" during the recording process. I'm present at *United Sound Studio during Parliament-Funkadelic's historic 1978 recordings "One Nation Under a Groove" and "Not Just Knee Deep" as well as Larry Frantangelo's solo instrumental piece, "Brettino's Bounce" named after his son. It becomes a Parliament-Funkadelic 45, a rare occurrence for a Warner Brothers' release. The song title is even adopted as the name of a stout beer made at Franklins Brewery in Maryland. I become a familiar presence at *United Sound and rent rehearsal space for *Dan Lewis and Friends even after the studio is sold.

My own recording sessions during the late '80s and early '90s continue to sharpen my ears and increase my objectivity about how my band actually sounds. The process demands precision and attention to the composition. Exposure to sound engineers and producers teaches me discipline and draws out my capabilities, even those I'm unaware that I have. The studio environment provides a canvas for creativity, and I appreciate being able to correct anything, opportunities that aren't possible during a live performance. I'm allowed to sculpt an idea with the support of highly skilled ears and know-how. It allows me to flex my muscles as an artist and a musician. I'm not a session *cat and have never claimed to be, but studio sessions put me in touch with creativity and familiarize me with different ways of doing things. Above all, recording provides a mirror that shows me what I'm delivering. I can step outside myself and peer back at my performance. It's a humbling look at oneself, and I'm never completely satisfied with my tracks. Ironically, studio experience exacerbates one of my greatest weaknesses, the quest for perfection.

Hooker 'n Heat (album by Canned Heat and John Lee Hooker)

My good fortune in meeting two blues greats, Bob "The Bear" Hite (1943-1981) and John Lee Hooker (1917-2001), is owed to Russ Gibb, Detroit's *Grande Ballroom operator and concert promoter, and my dad.

Russ allows me to enter the network of insiders at many performances, this one by Canned Heat at the Masonic Temple. I'm backstage talking to singer Bob Hite, blues historian and record collector, an artist who probably knows more about American blues than anyone I've ever met. When I mention my appreciation of Canned Heat's authenticity, it leads to conversation about John Lee Hooker's adaptation of electric-guitar-style Mississippi Delta blues. I tell him John Lee is one of my heroes, and of course Bob knows much about the blues legend.

Soon thereafter during a 1970 trip to Toronto, Dad takes me to a bar where John Lee Hooker is performing. John talks with me between sets. I tell him I'm a musician and that he's been a huge influence. As we talk about the blues genre, he says, "You live the blues. Keep on goin'." I tell him I recently spoke with Bob Hite of Canned Heat who shares my admiration for him. He winks, smiles and tells me, "Gonna do an album with Canned Heat (*Hooker 'n Heat*, released 1971). Those White boys got their shit together. They're my boys." He goes on to say that he likes the lengthy variation of his tune "Boogie Chillen" that they do at the end of their concerts. "They do me proud. They've got the essence of my brand of blues, and I'm grateful."

When I tell John Lee that I'm from Detroit, his eyes light up as he tells me that so many great blues and jazz musicians are from Detroit, a music mecca. "There's something in the air that you can feel. The city has deep cultural heritage and great blues legacies." Then he adds, "Say hello to my friend Johnnie Bassett."

♫

Related note about Russ Gibb and Detroit's blues legacy:

Russ shared a special treat with me, some tapes he obtained from the brother of Detroiter Sippie Wallace. This was before Sippie was introduced to a new White audience by Bonnie Raitt and others including Eric Clapton and Mick Jagger, bringing Delta roots artists into broader view.

Room to Grow

Ernie Rodgers knows I have big ears and a passion to perform. He tells me, "It's not how many chops you have. It's how the music is heard." There's solid mentoring going on here at the Rodgers family's *Rapa House, an after-hours setting for Detroit musicians. It's an environment where I can stretch my stride as a percussionist during night-long jam sessions. I come here to listen, play and broaden my exposure to improvisation. Musicians frequent Rapa en route to becoming studio musicians or playing in symphony orchestras. With the encouragement and collegiality of the musicians at Rapa House in 1977, I learn to hold down my part of a composition and work on fitting into, and being consistent within, the rhythm section. I become increasingly confident of my ability to contribute to the music and learn to apply my capabilities and extend my potential in spite of physical challenges. It's here that I'm exposed to a robust jazz vocabulary. It's here that I develop the unrehearsed responses that are necessary during a live performance.

At this writing, I realize that I should have invested more time and energy exercising and building physical stamina when I was a young musician. It's especially important for a percussionist. Even in the supportive environment at Rapa House, there were moments of frustration and anger when I was told, "You have to push yourself." Strength and energy transmit power. Mental and physical states are entwined.

Bringin' It Home

> I like the communication and trust that comes
> from a long-term relationship.
> When you know musicians as people,
> you feel you can really count on them.
> That frees you to take more chances and...
> it takes the music to a higher level.
>
> *Dave Liebman*

We talked about the potential for Detroit gigs on the night in 1980 when I first met Dave Liebman at *Seventh Avenue South in New York City (Chapter 3: Up and Down the Staircase, section Music Vortex). That meeting was auspicious. You never know where an adventure will lead, especially when it involves friendship. I'm so glad I took a chance on going down those rickety stairs into a dimension where jazz wizardry happens.

At my first performances with Dave in 1982, we sell out two shows at *Clutch Cargo's in Detroit (not the one in Pontiac). The group includes Dave Liebman (saxophone), Joe LoDuca (guitar), Gary Schunk (piano), Ken Kellett (bass), George Bennett (drums), and Larry Fratangelo and myself (congas and percussion). Dave's consummate professionalism drives the performances. He's in command of the audiences who become absorbed by masterful, non-stop delivery.

Dave Liebman amazes me in the way that I've been amazed by avant-garde jazz *cats Cecil Taylor (pianist), Derek Bailey (guitarist) and Anthony Braxton (saxophonist). He provides me with the recipe for improvisation and teaches me about responsibility in applying its principles. You must first understand the form and know the changes. From Dave I've learned to be daring and creative but in tandem with those who are playing with me.

Brassy Blues & Beyond

The music of Paul Butterfield (1942-1987) has been a mainstay dating back to the days of my imprisonment in elementary school and the daydreaming that helped me get through it, staring out the window at the playground and imagining I was listening to "East-West," "Driftin' and Driftin'" or "Two Trains Running." Butterfield introduces brass into some of his tunes in the '70s, such as on the album *Better Days*, changing and advancing the sound, fusing blues and jazz. Rock 'n roll is less sophisticated. It doesn't rise to this level, and I'm realizing that straight-up rock 'n roll exists in a comparatively shallow pond. My ears are opening to symphonic arrangements. The music of The Paul Butterfield Blues Band is bending my preferences in the direction of orchestral sounds long before envisioning the big band sound of *Dan Lewis & Friends.

After all the years of listening to and idolizing him, I finally get to meet Paul Butterfield in the '80s at *Alvin's on Cass Avenue near Wayne State University. Three of the guys from Paul's '70s band, Paul Butterfield's Better Days, are native Detroiters who have moved back here: Rod Hicks (one of Detroit's premier bassists who died in 2013), George Davidson (drummer) and Teddy Harris, Jr. (1934-2005, pianist, soprano saxophonist, composer, arranger). They're all gigging with various groups, as do most Detroit musicians, giving me the opportunity to meet them. I'm elated about getting to know these *cats. Teddy Harris, Jr. occasionally lets me sit in with his big band at *Bo-Mac's Lounge. I'm blown away by having an opportunity to play with musicians I've admired for so many years and even more so by getting to know them as friends.

Universal Language

Music happens to be an art form that transcends language.
Herbie Hancock

Larry Fratangelo is in seventh heaven when he arrives at *Metro Music Cafe' where I'm catching a meal with Al Jarreau before his performance at the Fox Theater. Larry is accompanied by Los Munequitos de Matanzas, a Cuban drum troupe that has just performed at the African American Museum. Their music is total catnip for Larry, a seasoned percussionist with a passion for world music. Larry begins tapping out a rhythm on the table. The conversation is challenging due to the language barrier, and the Cubans are becoming loud, animated and aggressive in their attempts to explain *Montuno *Guaguanco' tempos. In an attempt to subdue the agitation and what is sounding like an argument, Al stands up and tells everyone (not that the Cubans understand what he's saying), "Man, you guys are too heavy for me. You need to chill out. Why don't you take in a cartoon or a movie and relax?" Then he bursts out in laughter, and off he and I go to his concert at the Fox.

After Al's show, I head to the Atheneum, a hotel in Greektown where Larry is still with the Cuban drum troupe. Up in one of the rooms, percussion exploration is taking place, and I can feel the vibrations in the hallway before entering the room. Serious shit! Complex, heavy rhythms—*Guaguancó, *Batá, *Clave and *Merengue—with over-corrected tempos and variations on improv solos. They're communicating without spoken words through Afro-Cuban drumming, like the messaging between African villages. As my grandfather taught me (Chapter 7: Avalon, section Grandpa and Me), language isn't necessary to communicate. I see the glimmer in Larry's eyes. He's in his element with this percussion troupe from Havana. And I hear the unforgettable rhythmic artistry with my own ears.

To the Apex and Back

I arrange a performance by *Dan Lewis & Friends featuring guests Dave Liebman and Rick Margitza at the 1990 *Montreux-Detroit International Jazz Festival through festival director Jim Dulzo who's open to ideas, willing to listen, and knows how to support a vision. I've worked hard to bring my band to this apex, so powerful, impactful and plugged into the muse. It's one of the best performance experiences of my life, and it's with world class *cats. The group includes Walter White on trumpet, John Dunn on bass, Bob Tye on electric guitar, Al Ayoub on acoustic and electric guitar, Gary Schunk on acoustic piano plus a battery of electronic keyboards, Larry Fratangelo and myself on electronic and acoustic percussion, Rick Margitza on tenor saxophone, Dave Liebman on soprano saxophone, Mark Kieme on bass clarinet and tenor and soprano saxophone, and Dave Taylor on drums.

The streets are alive with people—4,000 of them. The performance is filled with rare moments. Energy and balance, just right. All musicians give and receive mutual respect but beyond that, there's communication without words and seamless interplay between all of us as another power takes over. We perform Miles Davis music plus compositions by Dave, Walter and Rick. We become reflectors, channelers. When you play fusion, it can go on and on and on, so a 1--hour set really isn't much time. We draw the audience in and keep them. These are the moments every musician lives for.

> **Sometimes when it goes really well, you wonder,**
> **who's at the piano?**
>
> *Cecil Taylor*

We receive a standing ovation, and I can feel the energy emanating from the crowd. As an encore, we play Miles Davis' "Tutu." I'm imagining where it would lead if this group of musicians could perform together all the time.

*Baker's Keyboard Lounge

"Should I hire so-and-so?" Clarence Baker isn't an easy guy to get to know, so I'm honored each time he asks for my opinion. I've been a fixture at Baker's since the '70s, so by the '90s my relationship with the owner is familial. He asks my advice about potential performers, some of them having national reach and beyond. He wants to schedule talent that will yield a maximum profit as well as the best quality. Clarence is a businessman with standards for how Baker's Lounge is run. Over the years, he sells the place several times on a land contract only to take it back if he's dissatisfied with the state of operations.

When *Dan Lewis and Friends plays at Baker's, I'm so caught up in the music and excited to be on this legendary stage that time is suspended. I get lost in the performance, losing track of time during extended solos that result in the band playing overtime. Clarence tells me, "Jesus Christ, Danny. Give your band a break. You're playing them to death." There's never any mollycoddling with Clarence, but I always feel at home. Once you break through his hard shell, there's loving acceptance inside.

New Opportunities

In the early '90s, Al Ayoub tells me that Phil Marcus Esser, a folk singer whom I've admired since hearing him in the '70s at the *Raven Gallery, is adding some percussion. I never imagined that I'd someday perform with him, but as it turns out, I do. Folk music requires me to learn a different way of delivering. I approach the songs from a band perspective, keeping things tight and sticking to a tempo. This irritates Phil, and I'm soon to learn why. From him I learn that folk musicians are storytellers who don't play a song the same way twice. Their tempo fluctuates, and even if you've rehearsed it a certain way, it will probably change during the performance. When it does, it becomes my challenge, not his. Phil teaches me to let the tune be the vehicle, and the folk genre shows me how musical feelings can float unencumbered, allowing me to add my own signature while a song is delivered in varying ways.

Through Phil Esser and Al Ayoub, I meet Detroit Mayor Dennis Archer who's friendly and supportive. He opens doors for me when I place bids on gigs, calling me at home a couple of times. My dad tries to act unimpressed as he informs me, "Dan, the mayor is on the phone. Don't keep him waiting." It's also through

Phil and Al that I meet Father William Cunningham and Eleanor Josaitis, co-founders of Focus: HOPE, and *Dan Lewis & Friends plays at the benefit for two years.

In Awe of Elvin

Dave Liebman invites me to take part in a panel discussion, an Elvin Jones tribute in a talk tent during the 2017 Mack Avenue Jazz Festival in Detroit. Like Dave and some of the members of his band, I've had the honor of actually knowing Elvin. As a panel, we share memories of a legendary jazz drummer who delivered pure melody on drums. Elvin's compositions and performances had no boundaries. He played out front, loud like a freight train but within orchestral movements, using his instrument to make the music a higher endeavor. He "felt it" like the quote at the beginning of Chapter 8: Are You Listening? "Some people feel the rain. Others just get wet." Tuned-in listeners could feel it, too, when Elvin Jones played, at times pounding and at other times gently showering, cascading over a wide range of beautiful note choices and melody lines. I'm in awe of musicians who not only feel it but bring it, as Shirley Horn (Chapter 6: Escapades & Escapes, section Takeout Preferred) described when she told me about her experiences with Miles Davis when he used chord phrases to broaden sounds and create nuance.

During this panel discussion, time is wasted on irrelevant information, the moderator missing opportunities to pose questions to Dave and his group about their real-life experiences playing with Elvin. Their observations and insights would add so much to the discussion.

Hearth and History

Call me crazy or perhaps it's as spiritual as I ever get but I can feel the life force of this city [Detroit] emanating from its buildings and oozing up through its streets.

Abe Sulfaro (1970-2014),
musician, author and poet

I admit having mixed emotions about Detroit. It's where my roots are and the home of so many friends and musicians who are dear to me. And yet there's some disdain on my part, partly because I was stuck here during the socioeconomic apocalypse when the city's glory died on multiple fronts. It's the place where I've needed to remain, in the care of those around me. As for the music this city is best known for, I don't put it on a pedestal. As I told Martha Reeves when she was extolling the greatness of Motown music, to me it's the pop stuff people listened to when they were making out in parked cars in the 60s. Truth is, Motown isn't my groove music, but without question it has touched Americans and people worldwide in positive ways that cross racial, social and cultural boundaries.

There was something present in the culture of Detroit when I was growing up, particularly within the community of musicians. My mom would chauffeur me anywhere and drop me off, or she'd load my equipment into a cab and send me off to music events and venues without too much concern about my safety. She knew there were guardians and protectors watching out for me. If I was invited, no questions were asked by my parents; they packed me up to go. Detroit musicians were my family then, and they still are. I'm reminded of the cradling atmosphere within the music community of my youth as I listen to an interview with Leonard King (video documentary, *Visger Road Revisited*, 2015). He describes the nurturing folks who surrounded him, a 12-year-old fledgling drummer who later became one of Detroit's jazz pedagogues. Leonard absorbed those values, to this day stewarding excellence, preserving music legacy and mentoring others.

In the '60s, Detroit was rich in live music venues. It was also packed with some of the greatest multi-talented singer/songwriter/producer-types in the country including Lamont Dozier, Norman Whitfield and brothers Eddie and Brian Holland. Musicians could make a living playing seven nights a week and doing session work.

As for the recording business, my bias was in favor of *Fortune Records, a family-operated label. It had a huge impact on Detroit music but was commercially overshadowed by Motown. Fortune's recordings weren't watered down for the sake of production. They'd do a few multi-tracked takes and in doing so captured a certain authenticity with less emphasis on production. The artists shine on those recordings. *Fortune's R&B records spoke to me, yielding the real urban experience, straight out of Detroit's melting pot, much of it eclipsing the music on the Motown label. One of the kings of these recordings was Nathaniel Mayer, a.k.a. Nay Dog or Nate. I'm also a fan of Spyder Turner with his version of "Stand by Me" and Nolan Strong's "The Wind." Fortune was diverse. It included R&B, blues, soul, doo-wop, pop, big band, hillbilly, gospel, rock 'n roll and polka. *Impact Records also had an impressive list of artists and recordings and has been described as a powerhouse of garage, pop and soul singles. Their artists included Mitch Ryder & The Detroit Wheels, The Human Beinz, Mickey Denton,

The Boss Five, Shades of Blue ("With This Ring" and "Oh How Happy"), The Classmen, The Sheppards, The Inner Circle ("Sally Go Round the Roses"), Sincerely Yours, The Lollipops, The Sixpence, and Rodriguez, a.k.a. Sixto Rodriguez or Jesus Rodriguez or Sugar Man as in the film about him.

The full landscape of the recording industry in Detroit reflects how the largest and sometimes predatory companies suck up all the oxygen. When Detroit music is mentioned, most people recall Motown, the hits its artists produced and those who attained star status under that label. Few other Detroit labels had the staying power that Motown had, and they didn't become the giant that Motown became. Berry Gordy was a brilliant marketer, but the music legacy of Detroit is much broader and deeper than Motown.

Berry Gordy ran an assembly line of artists, not all of whom achieved top tier status because they weren't given hit material, not that this wasn't and still isn't the case with other record labels. There were many greats who existed below the top tier and are seldom mentioned or acknowledged including Janie Bradford who co-wrote "Money," soul singer Gwen Owens and Berry Gordy's sister Anna Gordy Gaye (married to Marvin Gaye 1963-1977) with her label, Anna Records. Outside the Motown label, some Detroit artists who sprung into the national and international spotlight are Barbara Lewis ("Baby I'm Yours"), Aretha Franklin, Deon Jackson, Gino Washington, J.J. Barnes, Spyder Turner, The Capitols ("Cool Jerk"), Tim Tam & the Turn-Ons, Little Carl Carlton, Soul Brothers Six ("Some Kind of Wonderful," later a hit for Grand Funk Railroad), Freda Payne, Little Soul Brothers and Lonette McKee. At the same time Motown was dominating Detroit and national charts, there was a lot of great music being recorded elsewhere such as at *Chess Records in Chicago and the music coming out of Philadelphia.

Seeking opportunities in the film industry, Berry Gordy moved Motown Records to Los Angeles in the early 70s. Prior to the move when rumors began to fly, Motown denied it. When it actually happened, some of the bread 'n butter back-up talent (the Andantes, Marlene Barrow, Jackie Hicks) were abruptly abandoned. These were songwriters and singers whom the producers loved because they brought a signature style straight out of the African American church with interplay between lead singer and choir. They created impromptu arrangements and could lay down tracks in minutes. Some of them weren't paid for work they'd done when Motown moved out. Can't respect that.

There are many fond memories of *United Sound Studio. From the late '70s into the '80s, percussionist Larry Fratangelo recorded with Marilyn McCoo, Anita Baker, Funkadelic, The Dramatics, Albert King and many others. I accompanied Larry and sat next to producer Mike Powell during the recording of Anita Baker's breakout album containing the hit singles "Sweet Love" and "Caught Up in the Rapture." It was an unforgettable experience filled with Grammy moments. After United Sound Studio owner-producer Don Davis sold it, the business folded and was abandoned for years. The people who later purchased the building recognized its historic value and decided to make it a landmark and a museum. Preparing for the grand opening, they assigned a secretary to call members of the old guard—names on a list—to attend. Larry was invited, and I went with him. Apparently no one took the time or interest to connect names and faces with the music history that took place inside United's walls. Not realizing that Larry was on many of the records displayed on their wall, he was asked, "Who are you?" Being the good friend that I am, I started laughing at his expense, thinking to myself that perhaps they should have provided name tags. This perceived (however unintentional) affront might seem egotistical, but the question is just one example of hometown musicians being without glory in their own land. So many people don't bother with history or context, but it's particularly ironic at a museum.

Maybe it's human nature, but many Detroit artists have been reluctant to venture beyond their familiar zone. The longer you stay, the longer you stay. In contrast, Regina Carter, James Carter, Rick Margitza and Rodney Whitaker got out because they knew the music business had migrated to where the scene bustles— New York City, Los Angeles and Nashville. So did Detroit jazz singer Judy Roberts, saxophonist Bennie Maupin, bassist Don Fagenson (who became producer Don Was), vibraphonist Milt Jackson, bassist Ron Carter and guitarist Kenny Burrell. The necessity to make a break from home turf is nothing new and will continue unless Detroit once again becomes a music industry hub. The importance of residing where the music is produced was emphasized during a 1982 stay at the Nashville home of drummer Larrie Londin (The Headliners, Motown 1964). I remember him saying, "Some people think they don't have to move to the music scene to increase their reach, but the truth is they do. You have to move where the business is and take your confidence along with your instrument." The most successful artists who are from Detroit—and there's a lot of street cred in being from this city—have had the drive and confidence to seek broader career landscapes. They include Ray Parker, Gino Washington, Lonette McKee and jazz drummer Gerald Cleaver. There have been a few more recent exceptions to the stay-put tendency including

Eminem and Kid Rock, the Motor City being their springboard to national fame and film opportunities.

While I'm smackin' on hometown peeps, here's another observation about Detroit-based artists as compared to those in New York City and Chicago. Non-Detroiters are faster to respond to inquiries and requests for performances. In my experience, they readily return calls and take care of business. The general point of view in New York City is "If you're slow, you blow." They know how to hustle within a crowded jungle, and they're more willing to consider small jobs. Everything is important. A gig is a gig.

CHAPTER SIX
Escapades & Escapes

If you don't live it, it won't come out your horn.

Charlie Parker, a.k.a.
Bird, a.k.a. Yardbird

Smoke and Snake Oil

The air is hazy, and the funky aroma of weed wafts out the door as we enter the apartment at a brownstone in *SoHo in 1979. Having some time to spare before meeting up with Elvin Jones at *Village Vanguard where he's performing, drummer George Bennett and I decide to drop in at a get-to-gether where a mutual friend, clarinet player Perry Robinson, will be. I admire Perry's musicianship and hope he'll play a bit! Sure enough, he's here amidst about a dozen barefoot, stoned hippies with flowers in their hair and a bearded guru named Ali Baba (could he be more original?) who is dressed in a full-length white robe, drinking Miller beer from a can—the first clue that he's peddling phooey. There's a vintage clawfoot bathtub in the center of the room, but it isn't connected to water. This place is like a scene from a Woody Allen movie, packed with real-life caricatures.

It's soon announced that Ali Baba will conduct a jam session. All right! I'll get to hear Perry on clarinet. Everyone is getting higher and higher, and I take a couple of drags off a joint that's being passed around. I'm assigned to play tambourine. As Ali Baba distributes some percussion instruments, he's extolling the importance of modulation. Really? That's the second clue that this is phony baloney! It seems I'm getting real while everyone else, with the exception of my friend George, is getting way out there. The jam session gets off to a jerky start, arrhythmic and dissonant, and doesn't last more than a few minutes because the "musicians" aren't totally plugged into reality and Ali Baba has no fucking idea what he's doing. He quickly realizes that he needs to avoid being exposed, so he raises both arms in a comical supplication to some spiritual entity and then abruptly drops them to his sides as if he's conducting the dramatic end of a musical score. The performers, who at this point aren't even loosely tuned in to place and time, are smiling as they look questioningly at the guru. He appears to be waiting for some indication that they're even vaguely aware of how awful their music sounded, but they're trippin' now and continuing to smile, beyond feeling offense or shame as Ali Baba attempts to admonish them for what else but their lousy mod-u-la-tion, enunciated loudly as if he's speaking to hearing impaired fourth graders who are learning a new word.

Realizing that he's making a futile attempt to communicate with people who continue to look at him and smile, his eyes lock on me as he tells everyone, "Of everyone here, Dan, you really played well. Your tambourine sounded excellent." His feigned smile of approval is giving me the creeps. He's up to something to get his sham show back on track. The hippies are now dropping acid, removing their clothes and rubbing each other's bodies. In an attempt to maintain his command of the room, Ali Baba directs their attention to me as he asks, "Dan, how long have you been in a wheelchair? Would you like to walk?" The jam session conductor wannabe has re-entered his pseudo-spiritual element, and I'm feeling extremely ill at ease. In his most Maharishi-esque tone, Ali proposes, "We'll bathe Dan in oil, and he'll rise up and walk the streets of New York." Stating it loudly enough for everyone in the room to hear, I tell him, "I've lived with this my entire life," but drug-induced healers are locking their eyes on me. Sensing what's about to happen, I wheel myself as far as possible from the clawfoot tub. George yells, "Elvin is waiting at the Vanguard. We have to leave now!" He spins my wheelchair around, and we head for the door but are stopped by a big guy who's guarding it. We give him ten dollars to let us leave.

On the sidewalk outside, I exhale a sigh of relief. A love-in was about to turn into an orgy with me at its center. We catch a cab to *Village Vanguard and the Elvin Jones gig. Elvin notices that I'm somewhat shaken, so we brief him on the *SoHo jam session scene. He tells us, "You're here now, so no worries." Hearing real music performed by a master soothes my spirit and transports me back to my comfort zone.

Caravan (a composition by Duke Ellington)

The bus comes to an abrupt stop and suddenly I'm airborne—a human projectile, landing with a thud crosswise of the aisle. As usual, I've been given a top bunk on the crowded Funkadelic tour bus. I'm not injured, so no one is overly concerned. They brush my ass off, and like a piece of luggage they return me to my perch.

Larry Fratangelo doesn't give a damn that I'm handicapped and has no patience for fretting about comfort. He told me when he invited me, "It's sort of like camping. You'll travel like I travel." It's just a blown tire this time and not a breakdown that requires repair in a garage, a routine happening when the band is on the road for up to a year at a time.

I'm just glad to be on the road with George Clinton and this group of kickass musicians whom I met when Larry began to take me to *United Sound, picking me up in the morning for sessions that continued through the night during 1978-80. I'm always a welcome addition at the studio, never in the way, and George asks my opinion about his material. He has a come-one-come-all approach to art and work. He shares my interest in old R&B and my love for doo-wop, his roots growing up. He calls me "an encyclopedia," jogging my music memory and trying to trip me up on group names, dates and details.

Parliament-Funkadelic band members become a mainstay in my life during this period. They're invited to a barbecue at my parents' home on Grosse Ile. There's a lot of drinking, loud voices, laughter and funky-smelling smoke in the air along with the aroma of grilled chicken and burgers. There's no doubt that all this doesn't escape the attention of the neighbors in this stuffy suburban community, but Chuck and Suzanne Lewis couldn't care less. Dad becomes quite fond of Tyrone Lampkin (1948-1987), the drummer from New Jersey who sometimes stays at our house when he's in Detroit but more often at Larry's, even beyond the years with Funkadelic. Larry helps him find gigs. Tyrone is a gentle soul whose memory is treasured to this day.

If not for the Funkadelic experience, I never would have met Ron Smith of the Spinners. Many of the people I met then are friends to this day. I don't see them often, but when I do, it's old home week.

There's Something in the Water

Larry Fratangelo thinks I'm invincible. I should be on high alert when we're together—so many misadventures. There's plenty of time for a canoe ride on the river before dinner is ready at Larry's house, so we're sipping Crown Royal out of the bottle as he paddles. The current is unkind today, and the canoe is rocking, causing me to slip off the seat...or perhaps we've tipped that bottle a few times too many. When Larry tries to pull me upright while holding a paddle and the bottle of Crown Royal, the canoe overturns. As we tumble into the river, a plastic bag of hash falls out of Larry's overalls pocket into water. He reaches to retrieve it while hanging onto the Crown Royal with the other hand. I'm wearing a life jacket, but I momentarily become an underwater flipper swimmer, bobbing up to catch a breath. Only then does Larry grab my collar and pull me up where I can hold onto the canoe for dear life. It doesn't help that his glasses have fallen off, so he's blind as a bat. There's no question about his priorities. The first thing he says to me is, "Don't worry. The hash is fine," as he stashes the plastic bag inside his shirt.

Fortunately for us, a U.S. Coast Guard boat soon passes by. As they're hoisting us on board, my pants fall off. I literally have no ass, so my underwear slide off with the trousers. Boaters passing by find the scene entertaining and are beeping at the sight of my bare ass. A Coast Guard crew member who's lifting my pantsless frame on board yells at me, "Help!" as he motions that I should try to pull and climb up. He doesn't realize that I'm handicapped until I'm on deck. Larry and I are laughing, my face as red as the setting sun. As the Coast Guard watercraft approaches Larry's house to drop us off, we see my wheelchair where we left it—on the riverbank where I should have stayed.

To this day, Larry says, "We have to go canoeing again!" We talked last night, and he thinks it would be a great idea to go snowmobiling this winter. I told him, "No thanks. I've had enough brushes with death." Good ol' Larry. He responded, "Living on the edge is what it's all about, isn't it, Dan? There's nobody I'd rather die with."

Duppies (Malevolent spirits, Caribbean folklore)

Detroit drummer George Bennett and I hail a taxi in New York City in the mid-80s. It's evening, dark outside. We're going to have dinner with Edgar Winter and talk about some instrumental pieces he wrote (*Entrance* album, 1970). I'm hoping to record and perform them in a symphonic arrangement. Once inside the taxi, the driver turns and glares at us with an expression of disgust—or is it trepidation? In a Jamaican accent, he snarls, "When I saw you, I thought 'bout not stoppin' to pick you up. I don't like disfigured people." He's dead serious, and his tone is hateful. For reasons that include shock and speechlessness, I remain in the taxi rather than telling the driver to let us out, and we proceed to our destination. When the initial shock passes, I ask the him, "Why did you pick me up?" He snaps back at me, "I don't know." Intuition kicks in, and I get a sense that the driver's attitude is rooted in superstition or folklore. Perhaps there's a stigma attached to people like me? I'm wondering if he believes my condition is caused by evil spirits. Beyond that, I'm convinced that he picked me up to satisfy an impulse to belittle me.

The taxi pulls up in front of the address we've provided. Standing near the curb is an extraordinarily pale man with long white hair, white eyebrows, white eyelashes, and eyes glowing red under the streetlamp. I can feel the driver's reluctance as his foot presses the brake, as if he's experiencing an internal conflict over whether to stop or keep going. "Hey, Dan," Edgar greets me as he approaches the taxi and opens the rear door to help me out. The driver can't disguise his nervousness, and I can barely restrain the urge to burst into a voodoo chant as he grabs the fare and speeds away. I swear his complexion is lighter than when he picked us up. He's almost as pale as Edgar.

Takeout Preferred

Mark Murphy (jazz singer, Chapter 13: Melody & Harmony) and I are staying with Shirley Horn for a week in 1987 while Mark performs at a nightclub in the city. It's a memorable visit at Shirley's home in a rough area of Washington, D.C.

Shirley has a massive record collection, and I get lost for hours perusing it. Rap music has emerged from hip-hop culture, and I'm less than positive about the sound. Shirley hips me to the urban roots of the genre, explaining how it has grown out of a social and economic vacuum. There's no funding for music programs in ghetto schools. Kids don't have money for instruments or music lessons, so they improvise by using boom boxes, turntables used for "scratching" and their own poetry from life experiences. She predicts the scope and impact of rap, saying, "Music is going to change because of this." At this writing, not only is rap/hip-hop an international genre, but its artists are merging jazz and hip-hop using old *Blue Note recordings. I couldn't imagine at the time how prescient Shirley was.

I sleep on the couch and awake to the sound of Shirley at the piano in the morning. There are interesting dynamics at her place where her husband, Shep, waits on the diva hand and foot. The most invaluable moments are our conversations about Miles Davis who's "like an uncle" and Quincy Jones who produced some of her early albums. The highlight of my visit is getting to sit in with her during a performance at a D.C. nightclub.

One night after Mark's performance, Shirley drives us to a family-owned Chinese restaurant in her neighborhood. Over in a corner, there's a gang in a heated argument that's getting louder and louder and turns into a hold-up or a demand for pay-up. Suddenly guns are drawn and someone yells, "Everybody on the floor!" Everyone hits the floor except Shirley—and me, of course, because I can't. Mark, a gentle soul who always avoids trouble, slips out the door. I'm scared even though one of the guys tells me I don't have to get out of my wheelchair. Shirley is totally cool and unrattled. The only thing she seems to be concerned about is my food getting cold. She tells me, "Be cool, baby. Eat your food." I'm thinking, "Of course, Shirley, I'll just ignore the yelling, threats and guns and enjoy my chicken lo mein!" A grandpa in a house-coat and slippers appears on the stairs leading to the family's living quarters above the restaurant. He barks sternly in Chinese at the warring factions, and the dispute is immediately settled. It's apparent Shirley is a veteran, unfazed.

Shirley never moved from the poor neighborhood where she grew up, even after becoming world renowned. I hope I'm wrong, but I have doubts that artistry at Shirley Horn's level will exist again. She's in a class with Billie Holiday and Carmen McRae.

Missing in Action

*Dan Lewis & Friends with guests Dave Liebman and Rick Margitza have just finished a 1990 performance at the

*Montreux-Detroit Jazz Festival. I hook up with a couple of rep-robates backstage and end up at a hotel in a gleeful, night-long romp. Needless to say, the next day finds me in no condition to live up to an important commitment. Larry Fratangelo has a drum troupe, Chilla for Charity (speaking to the spirits of the universe through drums), and he has organized a 72-hour televised event that will feature over thirty groups. *Dan Lewis & Friends is scheduled to do a performance at 4:00 p.m., but by the time I realize that I'm going to miss the time slot, it's too late to make it to the stage. They announce my band—lights and cameras—and everyone except Dan Lewis appears. This throws Larry into a frantic scramble to fill a gaping hole in the line-up and places him in a hard spot with the news channel, not to mention the lack of consideration I've shown for my band members. To Larry's credit, he not only manages to fill the vacancy, but the groove continues uninterrupted. And what do I do? I go back to the festival and resume the weekend. Because Larry is a dedicated professional, the Chilla for Charity event is a success with percussionists performing, even between scheduled performances, for the entire three days.

When I see Larry a week later, he's still pissed and rightly so. In fact, he's so pissed that he grabs me by my jacket and slams me up against the car before taking me on a ride I'll never forget, making me think it's a ride to my death. He's screaming at me, the car swerving. I'm relieved when he stops at Charlie's Chophouse on Northline in Southgate. As if nothing just happened, Larry calmly says, "Let's get some lunch." Once we're seated at a table, he continues to behave as though he's cooled off, but no not me. Visibly shaken and indignant, I reach across the table and grab Larry who never has and never will make any allowances for my physical limitations. Taking this as an invitation to a rumble, he yells, "Let's go!" and before I know it, we're rolling on the floor in a brawl. I swear—only in Detroit—the waitress, in an attempt to break up the fight, gets down on the floor with pad and pen in hand, telling us today's lunch special. Larry pulls back, gets on his feet and lifts me into my wheelchair. He straightens my disheveled clothing, and we order lunch.

I was rude, thoughtless and irresponsible, showing no regard for my friend or the members of my own band when I failed to show up for a televised gig. Larry was angry with me for a long time, and I don't blame him. He still occasionally reminds me of my selfish, egregious behavior.

Saved by the Band

The atmosphere is electrifying at Armadillo's, a country music venue in Toledo, Ohio where I'm the guest of the James Michael Simmons (JMS) Band (Abe Sulfaro, Josh Sulfaro, Dan Oestrike, Billy Hamblin, Bob Olds). The house is packed, the music is loud and the dance floor is frenetic with strobe lights distorting the dancers. Lighting is dim here in the periphery where I'm sitting amidst tables that are mostly occupied by empty glasses because everyone is up and about with drinks in hand, talking and laughing.

I'm getting a creepy feeling that someone is staring at me and notice a man several yards away with his eyes fixed on me. He's trying to make eye contact, but I quickly look away. His stare is menacing, and I sense disturbing vibes penetrating the space between us. There are times when you just know you're in the presence of evil. He's a predator, and I'm easy prey. Each time I look away, he moves closer. No one except me notices or cares in this loud morass.

People who are having a good time drinking and dancing in a busy night club aren't going to notice this sicko who's slithering toward me. Over the course of about ten minutes, he has gradually moved within reach of me until I'm looking directly into his eyes. "You're coming with me," he says as he takes hold of my wheelchair from the back. I attempt to knock him away from me as people continue to walk by without noticing what's happening. I'm unable to completely turn around and hit him, so I'm flailing with arms that can't reach behind me and yelling, "No! I'm not going anywhere!" My struggle is going unnoticed in the noise and activity. I'm thinking this creep will abduct me, and I'll be found dead in a ditch.

Suddenly the entire scene comes to a screeching stop. The dancers are startled to a halt when Abe Sulfaro stops singing and yells into the microphone, "He's trying to take Dan!" He leaps off the stage and dashes across the dance floor followed by his brother Josh and Dan Oestrike. They rush toward the would-be abductor, and he escapes out an exit. They've saved my life. I'm sure of it.

Hurricanes

If I had my druthers, I'd live in New Orleans where rules are expected to be broken, or at least bent, and where people are likely to accept you on your own terms without judgment. Culturally, it's eclectic stew. Everybody plays by their own rules here, even the police. Mark Moultrup and I are at the 1996 New Orleans Jazz Fest because we want to catch performances by Herbie Hancock and Al Jarreau. We go into a bar where we befriend a topless dancer named Peaches, and she offers to show us the town the following day. We don't think she's serious, but she actually calls. Not wanting to appear ungrateful, we spend the next week in her company.

One night, a cab driver who's apparently envious of the good time we're having tells us, "I'm going to stop taking fares tonight and go drinking with you three." What a night! Mark, me, Peaches and a shiftless cab driver on a bar crawl. We're at O'Brien's when the driver asks, "Have you guys ever had a hurricane?" We answer "no." Over the next two hours, we each drink a few hurricanes. Mark picks up a paper and sees that Boz Scaggs is playing at the House of Blues. We ask the driver to drop us there. It's a small, intimate venue. Mark and I are given great seats, but once my wheelchair is in place, moving around isn't an option. I'm literally a captive audience—an inebriated one with an inebriated sidekick.

Four plump girls, one of them the size of a small dump truck, are standing directly in front of us. When Boz takes the stage, they don't take their seats. They're blocking my view as they gyrate their bottoms with arms flailing like they're in a mosh pit at a Cleveland rock concert. Considering the number of hurricanes in my bloodstream, I make a surprisingly polite request. "Would you please sit down so I can see?" They ignore me, so I try again. "I'll make you a deal. If you'll sit down, I won't mind if you stand during the encore." One of the girls in the middle shoots me a defiant look, and all four of them remain standing. I repeat the request two more times. They remain standing. On some level, I realize that we should call security to handle the situation, but the hurricanes are in control and I do something totally not okay and out of character. I grab one of the Miss Double Wides, the one directly in front of me, by the back of her blouse and yank it—hard. When it rips, she plops down and her friends sit, too. The second they're all seated, I yell, "That's what I'm talkin' about!"

After a couple of minutes, the four get up and leave. I'm hoping they just went to the bathroom...until security shows up with the one whose blouse I ripped. She demands that I leave or she'll press charges for battery. She and her friends have behaved badly, but her torn garment is proof of my aggression. I give her thirty dollars for the blouse, but still I'm asked by security to leave. Mark grudgingly leaves with me. Once outside, he yells at me, "Goddamn it, Danny! You really made a statement, didn't you? And now we're missing Boz Scaggs!" I yell back at him, "Oh yeah? If I hadn't made a statement, I'd still be missing Boz Scaggs from behind a bloated wall!"

Mark is pissed off and so am I, but rather than just call it a night, we shrug it off and proceed to another bar, no taxi driver and no Peaches. Always an adventure here, sometimes brought on by liquid stupidity, but I can't take sole responsibility for what happened. What were those girls thinking when they created their own mosh pit in a row of seats with others sitting behind them? Perhaps they'd had a few hurricanes.

Easy Victim

There's a sudden impact at the back of my skull, and the world around me goes black. It's a brief loss of consciousness but long enough for the mugger to pat me down. Awakening, I see the face of Buster Williams in a blur, staring down at me, holding my head up off the cement. "Hey buddy, are you okay?" From behind a foggy haze, I respond, "Uh huh." My mind is asking what the hell happened, and I'm not able to articulate anything for what seems like an hour or so. My last clear recall is wheeling myself toward the exit of the 2004 Chicago Jazz Festival where I've spent the day. Buster lifts me into my wheelchair and takes me to a first aid station, although I'm not fully aware of it until later. After tending to me, they offer to call an ambulance to take me to the hospital, but I insist on a cab instead.

I'm supposed to meet Mark Moultrup at the jazz club at The Blackstone Hotel where there's a who's who gathering of jazz musicians. Noticing that I look stunned and traumatized when the taxi door opens at the hotel, Roy Haynes and his girlfriend help me out of the vehicle and into the building. Once inside, Buster comes over to check on me, triggering clearer recall of what happened as I was making my way to the festival exit.

The thief didn't get my money because it's hidden in my shoe. This is my lot in life, caught between two options. Either I don't venture anywhere unaccompanied, or I do what I want to do, risking the possibility that some predator will take advantage of my physical handicap. The first option never wins...at least it didn't then, but nowadays (2021) I'm not as daring as I used to be.

CHAPTER SEVEN
Avalon*

The title Avalon is used here not only in reference to its primary meaning, the isle of fruit, but also as it relates to Arthurian legend with its tales of entwined human relationships, falls from grace, forgiveness and legacy. This family history is written with love, respect and gratitude.

Cliff Notes

I exit the womb in 1958 with cerebral palsy, dyslexia and an affinity for Ray Charles. I grow up in the Detroit suburb of Lincoln Park, and my family later moves to Grosse Ile, an island community on the Detroit River.

I never finish high school, not my scene. My experiences in the classroom could be compared with happenings in *One Flew Over the Cuckoo's Nest,* so at a young age I say "no" to school and "yes" to John Coltrane and Miles Davis. Rather than developing friendships with my contemporaries, I pursue music icons and

---

* Song by Roxy Music

legends—Van Morrison, Leslie West, Rod Stewart and other musicians decades older than I.

You don't choose music; it chooses you. It makes me feel special, like an adopted child. Music and musicians raise me, and Detroit provides the cradle and the playground where so many loves, musical and human, take root in me.

If there's such a thing as a normal range of challenges within a family unit, two children with cerebral palsy greatly expands it. I have two sisters, Debbie born in 1953 and Lori born in 1959. I'm between the girls, born five years after Debbie and 11 months before Lori. Like me, Lori has cerebral palsy however less severe.

At the core of our family is a father striving for success as a businessman and the financial independence that accompanies it. Chuck Lewis is determined to put distance between himself and his modest southern roots. His relationship with his father was less than good. Dad worked from the age of 11 and was motivated to prosper in a material way. He entered the U.S. Air Force saying, "I'm going to get away from all this." Once in the Air Force, he wasn't happy about having to take orders, but he earned the equivalent of a college diploma in architecture and left the service with an ambition to achieve the American dream. Pursuant to becoming a financially savvy suburbanite, Dad builds a lucrative commercial construction company and structures a life around pursuits and goals related to that status, but he has little self-discipline otherwise. He enjoys the lifestyle that's possible with what he earns. Even though my dad desires the appearance of a close-knit family, he really doesn't want to participate. He's an over-achiever with a restless nature, easily bored and never satisfied. Even after achieving his goals, he continues to pursue the dream, outwardly focused until it's too late.

My mother, on the other hand, tends to domestic priorities while also providing capable administrative and financial management of the family business. The amazing thing about Suzanne Lewis is the breadth of her abilities. When Dad starts his construction business in 1965 with outreach across metro Detroit, it leaves Mom as homemaker and caregiver for the children with the help of her mother, Lillian. Mom makes sure we're well cared for while she longs for a better family life...until she grows tired of holding out hope. Her upbringing by an eccentric father probably predisposed her to caring liberalism, a trait that serves us all well.

Dad builds all our houses, the first one in Lincoln Park. He frequently doesn't come home after work, so sometimes Mom doesn't bother to cook supper and my sisters and I go out for burgers or pizza. When Dad comes home at night, he and Mom fight. I hear them, and I'm certain Debbie and Lori can hear them, too. Our parents aren't in the same gear or even on the same road for that matter, so it's no wonder there's never a resolution to their differences. Every time the verbal battle reaches an inevitable impasse, one of them says, "We'll have to agree to disagree." I lie awake after their clashes, fretting and thinking irrational childhood thoughts, that if I don't go to sleep, maybe I can resolve the situation, or if I stay tuned in to what's happening between them, perhaps I can do certain things, or not do other things, to prevent their arguments. I'm never a totally carefree child, constantly evaluating family circumstances and looking for solutions as far back as when I was eight years old.

When my parents get along, they get along quite well. They take us on family vacations to Florida, Hawaii and other locations. Dad exposes us to gourmet cuisine in high-end restaurants on weekends. When Mom and Dad go on vacation together, Dad's mother and her second husband, Uncle Ray, stay with us. I'm crazy about Patty Duke, so they take us to see the movie *Valley of the Dolls*. Mom strives to keep the family environment stable, and Dad is the disciplinarian. Threats from him don't totally curtail my mischief, but they do rein me in. Respect is a value we're taught. Neither parent lets us falter when it comes to upholding behavioral standards, and they cut us no slack when we don't abide by them. Another value they instill in us is work ethic, Debbie and Lori both holding jobs from the age of 16.

1920s-1980s: Stranger Than Fiction

There are heartbreaking, extraordinary circumstances and happenings in this section about my mother's family. Some of it would sound extreme in the bluest of blues songs. I honestly doubt that a more tragic story exists.

Grandpa's mother (my great grandmother) was a morphine addict. Grandpa began hopping trains as early as five or six years of age, attempting to run away. From the age of ten, he pretty much raised himself. Coming from such a troubled, survivalist childhood, he wasn't a soft touch guy and often lacked awareness of a conventional lifestyle. It's no surprise that he was abusive in his marriage. Separation from my grandmother would have been inevitable even if their lives together hadn't been so tragic.

My grandfather worked odd jobs during the Depression. My grandmother was a housekeeper at the Dodge family mansion. In addition to my mother, they had three other children, a girl and two boys who all died within months of each other. One boy developed an inoperable brain tumor. While my grandmother was bathing him, his three-year-old sister opened the door of the house and wandered onto a train track and was run over. The other boy, seeing his aunt and uncle arrive for dinner, ran into the street to greet them while their car was stopped to make the turn into the driveway and was hit by an oncoming car. He was four years old. My grandmother's strength through the loss of three children came from her faith as a devout Christian Scientist. Understandably, my grandparents' marriage didn't survive. Rather than divorcing, they separated to avoid the humiliation and stigma associated with divorce at that time. Grandpa moved to a trailer park, and Grandma lived on Electric Street in Lincoln Park. She and my mother were best friends until Grandma's death in her early 80s. While walking to the market, she was killed by a 17-year-old driver who was impaired by drugs and alcohol.

1962-1973: Grandpa and Me

Having no solid grounding and being adrift in a world of many possibilities from the beginning of his life, Grandpa is a man of many interests and eccentricities including several dark obsessions. I'm a kid who has little patience with the usual childhood interests, so spending time with him is an intriguing adventure. Besides, he treats me like an adult. He allows me to cook with fire and lets me choose an adult book, *Valley of the Dolls*, which he reads to me saying, "A book is a book." My mom is accustomed to his ways and doesn't consider them bizarre. There are times when his temper is frightening, but he's mostly kind to me, does charity work for handicapped children, and shows me that there are kids who are worse off than I am. When I'm with him, I don't focus on the off-beat stuff. It's not until later that I learn about the tragic history.

I'm four or five. Grandpa takes me on walks in the hood to show me life outside the White suburb of Lincoln Park. If we go out for a burger or ice cream, it's a Dairy Queen, a Tastee-Freez, a White Castle or a Big Boy in a Black neighborhood. He often buys food for street people. On one outing, he treats me to ice cream en route a kids' Christmas event at Cobo Hall (now TCF Center). Hoping to set an example, Grandpa gets a small cone and tells me, "If I get you the large cone that you say you want, you have to eat it all." So of course I get a BIG ice cream cone. Back in the car, we notice some Black kids looking at us as we're enjoying our ice cream cones. Instead of buying the kids their own ice cream, Grandpa proposes that we give them ours, again hoping to teach me something. I don't want to give up my ice cream even though it's melting from the car's heater and running down my arm. Grandpa calls me a spoiled brat and smacks me— and not just once! He gives the kids our partially eaten, melting ice cream cones, and I get a lecture about giving to the less fortunate. Having just been smacked, lectured and deprived of my ice cream, I opt for the Black Santa at the segregated Christmas party at Cobo Hall.

During the years when I'm six to eight years old, Grandpa introduces me to the macabre. We read the writings of English occultist Aleister Crowley and obituaries in old, yellowed newspapers that are laying in stacks on his screened-in porch. He says, "News is news." We take long rides to off-the-beaten-path places. He never tells me where we're headed. If I ask where we're going, he always tells me, "Well, Dan, you don't know the party." It takes me a while to figure out that Grandpa isn't using the word party in reference to a fun event. He means a person or persons. The destinations are frequently cemeteries where we have picnics, discuss metaphysics and sorcery, and look at names and dates on headstones, figuring out how long each one has been dead.

At some of the graves, he says, "Now that's fresh dirt." We bring a lunch and relax in the quiet of graveyards during these eerie conversations. Grandpa also takes me to a lake where we collect interesting rocks in a bucket. He attempts to teach me, even with my uncoordinated hands, to skip stones over the water. I'm unable to skip a stone, but I'm not bored.

My grandfather has a look and a way about him that convinces people he belongs where perhaps he doesn't belong, such as the places we visit when his car crosses the Ambassador Bridge into Canada. He's fascinated by French culture and frequently visits French-speaking communities. We also visit Canadian indigenous settlements and take part in communicating with spirits through chants and prayer. The native folks don't speak a word of English and we don't understand a word they're saying, but they share meals with us and allow us inside their tribal circle because my grandfather approached the elders first. I especially enjoy the drumming and dancing. Grandpa has some Chippewa blood and my dad has Cherokee ancestry, so Grandpa predicts that I'll be a drummer. I enjoy these cultural experiences and learn to appreciate indigenous ways, but I don't yet fully appreciate what my grandfather is cultivating.

Grandpa admires Ted Lewis, an old vaudevillian. When he arrives to pick me up, he frequently uses Ted's emphatic opening line, "Is everybody happy?" He chooses a theme for each of my visits and rents or otherwise obtains films. He borrows the projector from Lincoln Park High School where he's the auditorium lighting director and sets up a movie screen in the living room of his trailer. When I ask where he got a particular flick, he responds, "You don't know the party, Dan." He's into old silent films starring Buster Keaton and Harold Lloyd. Grandpa explains, "You don't need the talking. The messages unfold before you." One example is a scene in which the main character attempts to hang himself by jumping off a building with a rope around his neck. He panics at the last minute, clinging to the hand of a clock on the side of the building as he looks down at traffic on the street several stories below. We watch can-can burlesque (strip tease) films featuring Sally Rand and Carmen Miranda dancing. Grandpa teaches me that the absence of voices can actually be better because it requires one to observe and interpret nonverbal meanings such as recognizing dance movements that communicate flirting versus lust and knowing that a person is refined by the way he/she holds a glass. He also enjoys watching mimes including Charlie Chaplin, and he tells me about vaudeville. Grandpa has an interest in the latest technology and is one of the first to own a reel-to-reel recorder and a color television. I'm into music on vinyl, 45s, so he takes me to see how records are made. We listen to recordings of Al Jolson, Eddie Cantor and Jimmy Durante. We also listen to my albums on his big stereo console that has a TV in the same unit. I bring Ray Charles, The Rolling Stones and other favorites. It becomes a music exchange between us.

At the Lincoln Park High School auditorium, Grandpa shows me how black light interacts with stage colors to produce unique effects. He researches lighting techniques and works with high school band director John Doyle to advance the level of productions, expanding the shows to include soul and R&B acts. They bring in entertainers who have hits breaking on the radio—Spyder Turner, Carl Carlton, Jumpin' Gino Washington and The Intruders from Philadelphia. Regardless of the type of production, Grandpa kicks it up a notch. Because of his relationship with the Canadian indigenous community, a full-scale performance that includes native regalia with headdresses, choreographed dancing, dynamic drumming and tribal singing is brought to Lincoln Park High School. The show takes place for three years running, having Grandpa's signature on it with varied performances from year to year, no repetition. I now wonder if this was his goal all along during our visits in Canada. When he leaves Lincoln Park High School, he takes on the same role at the Veterans Administration Hospital auditorium in Allen Park.

Among other things, Grandpa is a drummer. He gets down on the floor with me and bangs out rhythms. I repeat them, my first drum lessons. We go to the junkyard where he picks up items for our percussion laboratory in his living room. Various metals in the form of oil drums, hanging pipes, garbage cans and bells provide additional sounds, each one different. Because I'm in a wheelchair, he builds a wooden platform for the junkyard items so I can reach them. He gets me some drum sticks and mallets to use in our makeshift studio.

I'm Grandpa's audience as he rehearses with props for a magic show. He's an amateur magician, performing at schools and orphanages. He takes me to those shows and never misses an opportunity to point out other handicapped people. He's an acquaintance of Harry Blackstone whom he met at a magicians' convention. There's a combination of showman and the macabre in Grandpa. He's fascinated by Pagliacci, the tragic clown in the Italian opera, and considers the make-up process an art. He helps me put on show-biz-grade makeup and takes me to Monster Mash at the fairgrounds, an annual Halloween event for kids.

Grandpa takes me to the WJBK-TV studio where we watch the taping of "Morgus Presents" with Morgus the Magnificent, host of late night horror and science fiction movies who wears a long white lab coat, old sneakers and brown make up. He has long, straggly gray hair and bucked teeth. I also watch his afternoon spot when he does the weather report. Morgus becomes acquainted with us during our visits to the TV studio. We also get to know Detroit and Canadian radio and television personalities at WXYZ and CKLW including Mary Morgan, Bill Kennedy, news anchor Jacques "Jac" LeGoff, local actor Wally Fay, Captain Jolly, Johnny Ginger and Ricky the Clown. I really feel like a show biz insider when I see Ricky the Clown smoking cigarettes off camera! I dig Soupy Sales and watch his shows on WXYZ-TV. There's a children's show, "Lunchtime with Soupy," and a late night show where he sometimes has jazz musicians! I especially enjoy his waiter skits and tape his shows using Grandpa's reel-to-reel recorder. My mother's eye doctor golfs with Soupy, so a connection is made. He calls me at home a few times, even after he moves his show to Hollywood. During our first call, he's expecting to talk about his kids' show because of my age, but I'd rather talk about comedienne Edie Adams and actress Arlene Francis. I dig Edie and her catchy commercial jingle for Muriel cigars. I couldn't have foreseen that years later (1970s), Soupy and I would meet again when I played with the Johnny Trudell Orchestra at *DB's Club in Dearborn.

These are formative years when I learn to keep quiet during pre-recordings and live broadcasts as well as how to conduct an interview with a celebrity. Grandpa and I practice doing interviews and record them on the reel-to-reel. He teaches me how to listen through an entire response without interrupting and how to maintain the focus of an interview. He tells me, "I never learn anything when I'm talking." We go on location near Sault Ste.

Marie in Michigan's upper peninsula with naturalist photographer Ron Gamble who hosts an outdoors/wildlife TV show on Channel 4. While we're with him, he captures shots of birds in flight, and he and Grandpa talk about cameras and lenses. All these experiences plant a hunger in my gut for show business and radio. Like our excursions into French speaking and indigenous communities, I wonder how he slides us through the doors of radio and TV stations.

My grandfather and I shared many adventures from the time I was four years old until I was eleven. Our time together tapered off as adolescence approached and I became more and more immersed in the live music scene. He died of congestive heart failure in his late 90s. I now know that Grandpa's childhood subjected him to hardships that resulted in his unconventional but resourceful and creative approach to life. He either had no awareness of barriers and boundaries, or he refused to acknowledge them. I believe a life of survival on his own from such a tender age created the man he became. Knowing him enriched my childhood and has broadened my perspective as an adult.

Mid-1960s – Mid-1990s

Because of our closeness in age and both of us having cerebral palsy, my sister Lori and I attend nursery school together at the cerebral palsy center downtown on Brush Street. She's protective of me, aware that I'm not physically able to take part in all the activities. Then they separate us, believing that her helpfulness is impeding my independence, not to mention that Lori excels academically and should be mainstreamed. I remain in school through elementary and beyond, using escape into the world of music as a coping strategy. Dyslexia presents a barrier for me in the traditional educational setting, not to mention that the school environment runs headlong into my low tolerance for childhood and adolescent silliness. I never finish high school.

♫

The family business grows, and in 1970 Dad builds a sprawling 18-room waterfront home on Grosse Ile, an upscale island community on the Trenton Channel of the Detroit River. There's plenty of room for music equipment, records and jam sessions, and there's an elevator for me. My father can play golf more often here, and he joins the country club.

Mom can't keep up with the housekeeping. Neighbors on Grosse Ile have housekeepers, Black women from the inner city. Through those connections, my parents hire Mary Randall who lives up on Eight Mile Road, and she rides to work with Hattie, a neighbor's housekeeper. Mary dresses me, feeds me, and best of all, she sings to me—tunes like "Wade in the Water" and "A Change Is Gonna Come." She becomes my friend and protector. When I'm down, Mary lifts my spirits. She tells me, "One day you'll soar like a beautiful bird, Danny. You already are that beautiful bird in my eyes." I begin to see my life through Mary's struggles and her experiences with prejudice. She knows I'm dealing with prejudice, too. We share a love of the blues, and she hips me to gospel music. We talk about music and musicians—jazz, soul and blues. Mary tells me about the Regal Theater on Chicago's south side where she was born and raised. These are good times, and I can always feel the affection.

Between my mother, my grandmother and Mary, things always work out with the housekeeping and my care. When we move to a smaller house (1977), Mary's work with my family ends, but I treasure the memories of those days in the big house on the canal.

♫

My sister Debbie has a social nature. She looks outward toward friends and the examples they provide. She wants to grow up fast and seems to dance into things rather than having a deliberate plan. After graduating from high school, she marries at 19 like some of her girlfriends. She and her husband, Randy Hamilton, have a grand wedding at the country club on Grosse Ile, and Dad builds another house next door to the family home on Park Lane where Debbie and Randy reside and start a family. They have two children, Heather and Kevin. During this time, my niece Heather comes over to check on me from time to time when Mom is at the family business office. Then Debbie and Randy divorce. Having aspirations for a career in the culinary arts, Debbie becomes a chef and eventually owns and operates a delicatessen in West Bloomfield. She also she works as a chef in people's homes and provides on-site catering for residential events. She eventually moves to Atlanta, Georgia with her second husband, Michael Gorno.

♫

Lori graduates from Michigan State University with a degree in urban planning. She moves to Texas for about a year, returning to Michigan where she lives in Dearborn and then in Southgate, both locations near our home. Tragedy strikes in 1986 when her close friend dies of carbon monoxide poisoning while she's at his home. Lori survives after three weeks in a semi-comatose state. She doesn't use her college degree outside the family business, choosing to work for our father and later spending 17 years with a private mail and parcel delivery company.

In 1977, we sell the big house and move into a house on Park Lane, also on Grosse Ile and also built by Dad. In 1993, Mom calls time on the domestic situation, saying, "I'm not interested in spending the rest of my life like this." After 43 years, she stops holding out hope for change in the life of a drinker who justifies his behaviors with, "I provide for the family." That line doesn't work any longer, not that it ever really did. Years prior to this, I had accumulated enough experience to realize, as most men eventually do, that the man doesn't wield ultimate power in a household. Facing divorce, Dad has an epiphany and realizes that he can't un-ring the bell that he has been ringing for so many years in his family life. My mother, the stay-at-home business executive, is evolving through an interest in metaphysics. When Dad accepts that fact that the damage to his marriage won't be repaired, he starts spending more time at the family condo in Florida for good weather and golf. He eventually moves to Sarasota.

Mid-1990s - 2009

In spite of my family owning two remaining houses on the island of upscale abodes, Mom decides to make a clean break and relocates to a place where she can refocus. She buys a house in the middle class suburb of Taylor, sometimes referred to as Taylortucky because of the origin of so many of its residents who moved north to work in Detroit's manufacturing jobs. The previous owner of the house was a handicapped Vietnam veteran, so it's built on a slab without the need to construct an entrance ramp. Mom adds conveniences for me that include a wheel-in shower.

For a year while Mom is establishing a new residence, I live with Dad. Deteriorating health has caused him to move back to Michigan into the Park Lane house. He and I make trips to Sarasota for a change of scenery, and Dad builds Lori an apartment connected to Mom's house in Taylor. The year with Dad turns into a rough one for me, cohabiting with a father who's depressed, pitying himself and drinking. His desire to do his own thing without hindrance or inconvenience, plus a longstanding detachment from my daily realities, are apparent during an interaction that resulted in another eye-opener for him. He buys a new Cadillac every year, and it's being repaired. It will be out of service for four days, so he's without a ride to a golf tournament and quite miffed about being without wheels. I suggest that he call one of his friends for a ride. "You don't get it!" he responds. It takes no more than a moment for Chuck Lewis to realize that he's talking to a son who has to ask for help and depend on others for everything. The man who has never known a day without his independence apologizes. It's no wonder that he doesn't cope as his illness progresses.

Eventually Dad has to quit playing golf because of his health. He's miserable and bored, so we take trips to Toronto, Chicago, Las Vegas and Atlantic City to hear jazz and just to split the pad. When we're at Park Lane, we live like bachelors—flying by the seats of our pants, no regular meals and laundry piling up—two free-floating beings in the same house. Dad goes his way and I go mine. Mom makes herself scarce as she prepares another place to live. At the age of 32, I've achieved some notoriety as a percussionist. Like a gift that's delivered long past my desire to have it, Dad becomes interested in what I do. It's an opportunity for him, with the best intentions but also out of boredom, to get involved in my music, contacts and gigs. Fortunately, my longtime friend Larry Fratangelo is also living on Grosse Ile, so I spend quite a bit of time with him. When he's on the road, his wife Becky and I go out to eat and to events and concerts. I become part of their family and participate in activities with them and their sons, Brettino and Shaun.

As with everything else in my life, I view these circumstances through a musician's lens. Coltrane explores more than twelve notes. When he and his quartet take off, he goes out there. "Mary Had a Little Lamb" can step out its door and embark on an adventurous journey, but eventually the tune has to make its way back home to the melody. What I'm learning about form in music becomes relevant to my life. Improvisation in response to life situations allows you to change direction as needed, but there's still the inevitable return home. As a jazz acolyte, I learn to solo over complex chord progressions.

Life is like jazz...It's best when you improvise.
George Gershwin

I move to the house in Taylor with Mom. Becoming increasingly infirm, Dad moves into a nearby condominium. Mom is into metaphysics, so Susan enters our lives. She's an insightful and grounded spiritual counselor from San Francisco. She helps me understand that not everyone "travels" the same way, that there are portals to outside oneself, but you must be open to the windows and the journey. Susan brings insight and meaning to my life. I always feel positive energy, almost a current of electricity and a magnetic force, when she enters the room. Call me crazy, but during one visit, I see a yellow aura around her. It's the only time I've ever seen one. Susan speaks to my spiritual core, guides me to listen to my inner voice, and helps me plug into my power to get past self-doubt. She helps me much more than the credentialed childhood psychologists who neglected my spiritual self as they applied half-baked constructs. They always seemed to be trying to figure it out themselves, no answers, scraping the surface and giving me self-work to do. Visits to their offices left me empty and without hope. I know there are psychologists and psychiatrists who help people, but they didn't help me. Susan predicts an assisted living facility where I will stay for a while and will be tested. She says it will be unpleasant but that it will teach me about my own strengths.

As Dad's health continues to decline due to emphysema and cancer, Mom evolves spiritually. It's no surprise when she steps up to take care of him. In spite of everything, there's no question that they truly love each other. He died in January 2009.

2009 to Present

Changes take place during a ten-year period, subtly at first with Mom's frustration over trivial things. Lori is at work all day and Debbie lives in Atlanta, so I'm the first to become convinced of Mom's behavior changes around 2012. At first, I question my perceptions because of who Suzanne Lewis is, her brilliance, the woman who has been the interface with financial advisors and in charge of three family businesses. Then she develops obsessive-compulsive behaviors like reading every piece of junk mail and has temper outbursts over things that she otherwise would have ignored or taken in stride. She's anxious for unknown reasons. She forgets things and is frequently looking for lost items. She's unable to balance the checkbook. There are episodes when she lashes out, even becoming combative at times. I'm on eggshells with her. Debbie, Lori and I are all in some degree of denial, and none of us wants to accept what has become obvious. It's difficult to be objective when you're witnessing a decline in someone you love so deeply. Finally, an Alzheimer's diagnosis is made, and Debbie moves back from Atlanta to help care for Mom.

Everything is swirling around me. The last thing Lori and Debbie need is another person who requires daily assistance. I must consider alternative living arrangements. The emotional and psychological impact are devastating for my sisters and me. My friend Al Ayoub moves me into his mother's house where he, his wife and his sister are caring for his mother, and I stay there for a month until other lodging can be arranged. With Al's help, I move into an assisted living facility located a half mile from my mother's house, having frequent visits with her until her death in 2017. I'm now back at the house in Taylor with Lori.

Looking back over the years of our lives, it's clear how much Dad and Mom loved all three of their children, each of them making provisions for us in different ways. Dad had a business plan based on continual growth but no long-term financial plan. It was as if he thought, "I'll just make more money if we need it." He made the money and didn't hesitate to use it on our behalf. Mom allocated, invested and saved, having a stabilizing presence and vision that extended into the future.

Dad and I shared a sarcastic sense of humor, both of us smart asses. We laughed at each other, too. If I'm quick-witted, it's inherited from him. From my mother I learned generosity, willingness to help others, and principles about leaving things better than I found them.

Debbie has had reasons for her perspective and her choices as far back as adolescence and her teen years. At times she has appeared to have familial grievances and emotional wounds. Who can say how deep the impact was of having two younger siblings whose care, mine more than Lori's, required so much time and attention from our parents? I'll never forget Debbie preparing gourmet meals for my musician friends and the care she took in creating beautiful, delicious family meals on holidays. I'll always cherish these shared experiences with you, Debbie. I admire and respect your devotion to your children, Heather and Kevin.

Lori is a realist who doesn't need a lot of people for support and doesn't suffer fools. She personifies what most people aspire to, needing nothing for self-validation. Even with physical challenges, she never allows self-pity any place in her life, forging ahead with grace to accomplish whatever lies in front of her. She has taken me back into our mother's house since I left the assisted living facility, and as far as I'm concerned, she's not obligated. It's my good fortune that you help me, Lori. You're a bit of a perfectionist and fiercely independent. We don't agree on some things, so there are tense moments, but it all works out. You aren't easily impressed, and that keeps me humble.

Through all of this, I've become grounded and value the age that I am now. At 63 years of age, I have a seasoned perspective on where I've been and where I'm going, having learned many lessons and still trying to get it right.

CHAPTER EIGHT
Are You Listening?

Some people feel the rain. Others just get wet.
Bob Dylan? Bob Marley? Roger Miller?
Others...depending on the source

This chapter contains thoughts and narratives about auditory-cognitive listening (how I process music and place it on a relative value scale). It also contains lessons learned about quixotic beliefs and standards for the quality and purity of music.

Purist to What End?

Tending to be a genre purist, I must admit that I've been a slow learner in the "get real" dimension of the music business, particularly as it relates to artists pursuing commercial opportunities. What did I think they're supposed to do to make an adequate living? I've spent years thumbing my nose at pop and rock, considering them lower art forms, even kitsch.

After a manager put Edgar Winter and his brother Johnny Winter (1944-2014), a longtime fave of mine, on a rock music treadmill with the Epic arm of Columbia, I asked Edgar why, after so many years of jazz and R&B, he would sell out and record something like "Free Ride." He responded, "Why do you get so wrapped up in an artistic vision? Art and commerce don't have to be tied together." Damn. He was telling me that I don't see the difference in purpose. I had become enamored of Edgar's compositions on the studio album *Entrance*, believing then as I still do, that it's operatic, delving into life and human potential. Edgar helped me understand that the "other" music, the type that a genre purist places at a lower position on a relative scale, is recorded and performed not only because there are those who like it but also to pay the bills.

**I wasn't so interested in being paid.
I wanted to be heard. That's why I'm broke.**
Ornette Coleman

I'd also noted this happening in the careers of Rod Stewart and Al Jarreau. Rod was really good performing with The Jeff Beck Group and blues/rock-based Faces, and then along came Los Angeles music executive and record producer Clive Davis. The industry has a way of diminishing authenticity in favor of large-scale marketability. Who wants albums, anyway? Rock and pop promoters and record labels just want a couple of commercially lucrative singles. They aren't interested in a full-scale studio album like *Gasoline Alley* when they can sell a ton of singles with a "Maggie Mae." Al Jarreau, a real jazz *cat, attained broad reach when his star power was recognized. Then writers got involved, resulting in pop influence in the form of "We're in This Love Together" and the theme song for the comedy series *Moonlighting* starring Cybill Shepherd and Bruce Willis. My eyes and ears were again opened to reality by Al as described in Chapter Four: Elusive Expectations, section "After All." Various music genres are valid, the more commercial ones being done for a different audience and with a different purpose. You can have a preference for one without bastardizing or denigrating the other. When Skip Gildersleeve (guitar tech for well known bands including Kiss, Steely Dan and Rush) gave me a free pass to see Rush at the Michigan Palace, I reluctantly went, was unimpressed and ungratefully told Skip that the band was headed nowhere (WRONG!) as I rushed off to hear Chet Baker at *Baker's Keyboard Lounge.

There was another eye-opening conversation with Edgar Winter when he enlightened me about the non-exclusive relationship between pop music and what an elitist like me considers higher art. There were also interactions with Al Jarreau when he was considering recording the song "Let 'Em In." He told me, "Man, there's this great Paul McCartney tune...." He sang a few lines, sang them so well! The jazz nazi who lives in my head marched out. "Why? For money? Al, stick with your roots." My judgment was immediate—on my high horse—disregarding the fact that Al had already achieved some success with a version of "Mornin'" and others. He told me, "Yes. It's about making money, especially when you're working with a major label. What do you care? You aren't going to buy it, anyway." Man, did he ever have my number. As it turned out, he didn't record "Let 'Em In." Perhaps it's pretentious of me, but I still feel somewhat responsible. Like Edgar, Al was saying, "Dan, are you listening?" Yes, I get it, but still the connoisseur struggles with this.

Like everyone else, musicians have wide-ranging personalities and proclivities. When it comes to making money, they can fluctuate between artistic pursuit (wallet be damned) and unbridled grab-it-and-growl. As human beings, they float around in the boundless territory between humanism and hedonism if those characteristics can be considered opposing traits. My co-writer and I have had conversations about artists, musicians in particular. She was a teenager in the 60s and admits to having a tendency to place iconic musicians on a level with transcendent seers. She's smiling and chuckling at her own idealism as we write this, being reminded by me that artists are mere human beings, subject to all the trappings attached to that condition and just as apt as other people to be driven by worldly pressures and motives. Awareness of their humanity is the reason I don't become star struck.

Artists whom I admire stare into reality through a clear, wide lens and sometimes at great personal cost. They give us art that evokes thoughts and emotions, transporting us to fantastical places and expanding our consciousness. It's a gift that elevates humanity, the reason a price tag can be off-putting. Truth is, I still believe that music as an art form occupies a more elevated place than music as a commercial enterprise. But in the end, after years of deprecating commercialism, I also acknowledge it as a necessary means to economic survival, one that Edgar and Al taught me.

I've clung to a template called the *American Songbook, believing musicians should color inside the lines like Johnny Hartman and Mark Murphy. What a conspicuous contradiction this is for a guy who rebelliously rejects rules and boundaries. I guess in my mind, the type of rebellion that I live doesn't apply to music genre. But there's a further contradiction. I've long admired Beck Hansen as someone who jumps lanes, very eclectic, introducing people to multiple genres. He's one of a few artists who've broadened the horizons of young people and continues to be a trailblazer to this day.

Regardless of genre, if artists don't continue recording what is broadly marketable, touring and selling T-shirts and CDs into their golden years, they starve. At the time of my interactions with Edgar Winter and Al Jarreau, Edgar was signed with Epic (Columbia) and Al with Warner Brothers. Labels basically tell artists, "Make money for us or go away." This is one of the reasons only a few artists such as Bob Dylan and Johnny Mathis have remained with their original label over the long haul. Both of them were with Columbia.

Swirling Around the Zeitgeist

Many people are content listening to the same tunes over and over via satellite and online broadcasting companies like Sirius XM and Pandora. Those entities purchase blocks of tunes by well known artists, put them on replay loops listed by genre, decade or artist, and sell them on a large scale. In the meantime on other fronts, new and aspiring artists are told by corporate interests that they must sound like another group or artist whose music is making money. So much for unique sounds, artistry and forging new territory. As a result, serious and talented composers and musicians are doing independent recording, marketing and online sales that are more limited in scale.

Even though I get the difference in purpose, the fact remains that mainstream rock, pop and new country have become sound templates, repetitive and without depth or signature sounds.

Having broad (however shallow) appeal works for some artists who ride a short-lived wave. If a contemporary pop, rock or new country tune appeals to the masses, it's often not very good, and it's certainly not great. This sounds elitist, but I'm making no apology. I'm not blaming artists for what is pushed out in volume to the public, nor am I assigning total blame to big labels and marketers who are banking on what appeals to an undiscriminating public. It's circular. Preferences are driven by airwaves that are saturated with same-sounding shit played over and over and over. When low quality pasta is thrown at a wall of listeners who haven't heard much of anything else, it sticks. When it sticks, the industry makes money. Why would they do it any other way?

Have you ever been at a performance when the audience shouts requests for an artist's hits in a demanding, obnoxious way? It's as if they think the artist owes them the entertainment—delivered as they expect it. After all, it's what they paid for! The crowd tries to control the artist. Country legend Merle Haggard recognized that fans want to hear the songs they know and love, but he also took control when the demands interfered with his ability to carry on with a show in the way he felt he should. He told one audience, not in an angry or defensive way, that he was in charge of the performance. In the rock arena, it's party time, and the crowd wants head-banging tunes and special effects. My observation has been that crowds can be impatient and rude, ordering the artist to function as a human jukebox. I saw this happen at a Neil Young concert at the Fox Theater. Hits are catchy and familiar, tunes that have been marketed and sold on a large scale, but they aren't necessarily the best that an artist has to offer. Artists change and evolve in wonderful ways while the general public remains stuck where the artist began, having little interest in artistic evolution or new sounds that might unfold on stage. This was the case when Miles Davis migrated from bebop to jazz fusion and when Bob Dylan introduced electric guitar into folk music.

Granted I'm an outlier, having no desire to experience music solely as entertainment. I've nothing against it; it's just not for me. Rather than being lifted up by a full symphony in its innate glory, many people would prefer to be wowed by lights and special effects during a performance by Mannheim Steamroller or the Trans-Siberian Orchestra. I'm just saying it exists in a space where it's more about entertainment than the enjoyment of music. I believe it's this way for most serious musicians whether performing or sitting in an audience. All this being said, my co-writer reminds me that music and entertainment don't have to be mutually exclusive. I know there's an intersection, but I'm not interested in seeing Macbeth performed by soap opera characters.

CHAPTER NINE
Dissonance

All great art is a form of complaint.

John Cage

The title of this chapter reaches beyond sound. Something you'll notice in my life story is unresolved angst. Looking back at the years, I'm not sure whether I've felt sour grapes over an unfulfilled dream to be a regularly performing percussionist or whether I've been blind to the amount of wine in my glass, but it's probably both. I didn't like where I existed as a child, and I don't like where I am now. Rather than mellowing with age, it seems I've yet to settle in. There's perpetual unrest, always refueling and longing for some measure of contentment. The rhythm of life becomes syncopated as one catches glimpses of mortality.

During my formative years, the expectations of teachers and other adults, with the exception of my mother, weren't aligned with my needs or my interests. Too often their guidance and direction added to my struggles. Fortunately, I was drawn to another pursuit that was uplifting and fulfilling, one that transported me to another dimension, away from a life of physical limitations.

Its presence broadened and deepened my cultural and spiritual perspectives, but still I was surrounded and hemmed in by the packaged program. Finally, I had to get real about what was valid and valuable and what was not. I said to myself, "Look, jackass. You've got to stop listening to these people."

I discovered very early that it wasn't enough for me to imitate people.

Cecil Taylor

Straddling two worlds, I played at the *Wisdom Tooth on Plum Street with the Vernor Highway Blues Band at night and was back in the classroom with the other special ed kids the next morning. I wasn't interested in school, and a perceptual problem (dyslexia) compounded my frustration, leading ultimately to disillusionment with the school scene. It became an unwanted distraction. I preferred to venture outside the classroom where the lessons were of my choosing. When I was at school, I couldn't wait to get the hell out so I could chase my dream and pursue what was important.

I remained in school longer than I should have, from age 6 to age 22, thinking some miracle would happen and the trap door would pop open. During those years of being coaxed to forge ahead with conventional education, I began to weigh the daily struggles against the limited value they held for me. I finally figured it out. School was based on a widely accepted set of expectations that conflicted with my internal navigation system. I was trying to listen to adults and teachers and do their right thing, knowing that it wasn't right for me. If you're not good at something, and worse yet your heart isn't in it, why keep trudging along? School provided no way out for a kid who desperately needed to escape. It dragged me down spiritually. Didn't I have enough daily challenges without the school shit? I disengaged. By junior high, I was mainstreamed and used some dope to cope, returning from breaks and lunch feeling tranquil and detached. My noticeable indifference was perceived as withdrawal, and I guess in a way it was. They thought I was giving up when in fact I was saying "no."

I stayed too long at that fair, but trusting my own gut eventually served me well. I'm not dumb and I have free will, so I've managed to tune out insufferable squares with low cred. I won't live on their terms or be measured by their yardstick. My life is going to be a struggle, so I'll struggle my way. With few exceptions, I've proceeded on my own terms.

Becoming a solid musician is what I've always wanted, but limitations were predetermined by the circumstances of my birth. Some advised me to study music rather than perform it, but they didn't fully appreciate the extent to which dyslexia places academics beyond my reach. It felt like they were saying, "If you can't ride a bike, you'll just have to crawl." The truth is I don't mind crawling and would happily do so to reach my dream, but where academics are involved, I can't even crawl. In school I had to read the same line over and over, but there was no problem with my motivation to learn or retention of information. There was also a less than learning friendly environment created by a special education classroom full of kids with handicaps. Since those days in the classroom, I've done well with lectures instead of reading, and I've had a number of personal tutors. Fortunately, music is math, a subject that I can put to rhythm in my brain.

People are judged by achievements, earmarks of success. It's called "making something of yourself." Those markers usually correlate with notoriety or with money and what it can buy. Many believe that if you don't have a plan and stick to it, you won't have a financially stable future. I'm not saying there isn't relative truth in that belief, but there's little improvisation on the conventional pathway. The unconventional is considered risky or worse yet foolish. People get frozen in plans that are aligned with consensus expectations, few having the courage take an alternate path or travel to unknown destinations.

When herd expectations are thrust upon someone like me, the result can be painful and damaging, but I don't bend or break. I'm Rosa Parks at the back of the bus. Wonderful things can come out of refusal to be controlled and shaped. My body is messed up...gliding with a broken wing...but I'm not going to allow my mind to be messed with. I'm still minimized, but I refuse to be placed under a microscope and scrutinized. My ego is quite intact and sometimes too healthy. With bands and music projects, I strive to do things that allow me to say, mostly under my breath, "So, what do you think of that, mother fuckers?"

All this being said about the collective mindset and the conformity that I rail against, it's also true that I've felt I should be doing more to earn the respect and esteem of those who adhere to the generally accepted success standard. It's ego and insecurity on my part. What can I do to prove I'm as worthwhile as others? I'm hard on myself, and some would say it's irrational, unrealistic or even delusional. It gets in the way of personal contentment. When I'm minimized, it's usually because people pigeon-hole me. During circular dialogues with myself, I come back to the realization that I don't have to be judged by those who work 9-to-5 jobs to earn a living. I remind myself that I'm a builder of sorts, a resource, a connector and a facilitator who always leaves something better than I found it. When I haven't been performing, I've helped others. I like to think some of my ideas and efforts are beneficial, especially when I can help others discover who they are and where they're going in their music careers.

When people aren't fuckin' with the groove, they're jackin' around with perception. Doing so intrudes on precious moments and imposes uninvited beliefs and perspectives on one's in-the-moment experience. There's the hokey talk that goes on at the worst times such as following a death: "She's in a better place blah blah" and the crap about healing. To the healing jive, I just say, "No." Some people either haven't experienced it or don't understand it, but there is no healing after the loss of someone so dear that your consciousness overlaps with theirs. If and when I want to heal, whatever that means, I will, but marinating in grief keeps me in touch with my own humanity. Whether I want to move on or just allow the passage of time to lessen my sorrow, I'll do it in my own way and in my own time—or maybe never, thank you very much. I'll use whatever amount of time I need to reflect on what has come to pass in my life. So what if I want to sob uncontrollably or remain stuck in anguish longer than others think I should? It would be so much better if well-meaning people would squelch the words and just be present with you, allowing you to be where you are emotionally. The human condition might even evolve if just being present is learned and practiced.

It's not that I try to be a dark cloud or that I'm constantly in a blue funk. In fact, there are times when I could use a dose of downer to maintain a realistic perspective and control my own excitement, particularly when it comes to music projects. Discontent and grief otherwise keep me grounded. Some people prefer rose-colored glasses—happy, happy—and make it their mission to give you an emotional lift. Truth is, it's usually about them. They want your sorrow to be over asap for their own psychological comfort. Not only are people who are always smiling and cheery irritating, but I'm suspicious of them. They make the pricky blue jay who lives inside me want to come out squawking.

Too many people have an agenda that includes imposing their own values and preferences on others. They look forward to spaghetti and cannoli for lunch, and therefore you should, too. Spare me your New Year's resolutions. You're going to lose weight this year. Who gives a rip? I'm sounding like a contrarian or like I'm above it all, but people act like eight-year-olds. They put on party hats, break out the noise makers and insist that you participate. You must wear a party hat and have some champagne at midnight.

I'm not the only person, more specifically musician, who has faced challenges that, if allowed, would define me and box me into a place where little is accomplished. Neil Young comes to mind. He has had polio, a seizure disorder and a cerebral aneurysm. His left side, including his eye, doesn't serve him well, but look at what he has done artistically over the years. David Byrne has worked at overcoming a tendency to isolate himself due to borderline Asperger's Syndrome. He used to sit in a corner at social gatherings. He has had to force himself to interact. During a dinner conversation after a performance at Pine Knob, David told me that he now welcomes collaboration with others and that without it, your "own" doesn't reach full potential. In music, just as in other disciplines, it's simple. You must be in control of self and in synch with others to enhance the music without getting in its way. I learned this from one of the world's greatest saxophonists, Dave Liebman. You hang or you don't, and you do it without dwelling on limitations. I could waste a lifetime down the victim rabbit hole and never accomplish a damn thing. One must be fully cognizant of realities and responsible for his/her own life in order to move forward.

Bring on the Night (song by The Police, album by Sting)

As we're writing this section, it's early afternoon and I haven't slept for a couple of days. As evening sets in, I rise. My brain works better, more clearly, at night. Meaningful insights come to me after dark when I'm absorbed and the hours fly. Even then, I use low-intensity light. Sunrise entering through a window is irritating. It's been this way since I was a child who sat up at night watching talk shows. People discussing things are still more interesting to me than watching movies. Dyslexia probably has something to do with it. Deep sleep doesn't visit me. I wonder if REM sleep cycle disruption has negatively impacted my creativity, but a nocturnal biorhythm fits the life of a musician who does live performances.

Being told that I need sunlight, I've attempted to get into the swing of daylight hours. I've tried adhering to a daytime schedule because of the need to keep appointments in a world that operates by day. If I can keep daytime hours, it's more of a favor to others and holds minimal value for me. The last couple of years, my sister Lori and I have spent time outside in the summer, and I have to admit the exposure to vitamin D is good for me. But I am who I am, a creature of the night. I don't melt in the sun, but it does give me a headache.

Where Else but in a Chapter Titled "Dissonance"?

> It's like, how did Columbus discover America
> when the Indians were already here?
> What kind of shit is that, but White people's shit?
>
> *Miles Davis*

Only as an adult did I come to realize that there are patterned cultural and behavioral differences between races. White people talk too much, and they for sure give me too much advice even to this day. There are times when under my breath, I'm saying, "Shut the fuck up." Jazz saxophonist Wayne Shorter noted White Speak (not his words), the tendency to expound on fine points and damage the mystique. This irritating practice is also referred to as caging the butterfly. Whites also tend to talk and talk without a sense of timing, commenting on music while it's being performed and while the person on the receiving end of their chatter is trying to listen. Jazz trumpeter Sam Noto advised a musician who began verbally analyzing a piece while it was being performed, "Look, little brother. Save something for yourself. If you talk about it too much, it's a drag."

So there's that, but there's also the White tendency to think you have it all figured out even though you just learned of it—jumping to a conclusion without understanding the root cause and progression. It's an ignorant, know-it-all presumption that has resulted in much of the misguided advice that has been thrust upon me.

My Right to Exist

I'm alone at *Your Mustache Lounge in Dearborn. I often go to music venues by myself so that I can listen without having to interact with a companion, but tonight another kind of distraction begins tugging at my awareness—hostile glares coming from a man sitting at another table. Hatred is a strong emotion that jabs its way into your consciousness. I'm locked in place, trying to avoid eye contact. He repeatedly tips the glass to his lips, and I'm certain he's drunk. Bobby Lewis and the Cracker Jack Band are the reason I'm here. Their performance is where I'm trying to focus until the guy with the demonic stare staggers to where I'm seated, yelling at me over the music. "You know Hitler gassed people like you because he knew they have no place in society. They still don't!" His aggression is building, his speech is slurred, and I'm telling myself, "Shit. So much for some uninterrupted enjoyment tonight."

The best response from me would be no response, but it's difficult to ignore someone who's screaming at you from across your own table. I tell him, "I was put here for a reason, just like you." He spits out a toxic reply that can be heard over the music, and at this point he's grabbing the attention of everyone in the lounge. "You have no purpose!" Against my better judgment but because

I'm pissed and he's persisting, I counter him once more. "People like me are here to show that adversity is a part of life." At this point, he's leaning in toward me in a physically threatening way as he bellows, "I believe in getting people like you out of the way! The world needs a perfect race!"

The atmosphere is so tense that I barely notice when the music stops. The situation is out of control. People are frozen, mouths agape in disbelief that this Hitleresque dogma even exists in the year 1977. The guy is obviously unhinged and fueled by alcohol. Suddenly my wheelchair is backing away from the table. Bobby Lewis has left the stage and is pushing me toward the kitchen. Once inside, he tells me, "Dan, stay put until it's safe out here," and he disappears. It takes several minutes for the bouncer to escort the hatemonger off the premises. In the kitchen amidst steam, clinking glasses and pots and pans, the weight of what has taken place bears down on me. That man has challenged my right to exist.

Limit of Tolerance

In the early 1980s, Wayne State University and Michigan State University professors schedule me to speak to students about what it's like to be a handicapped musician. I can barely stomach it. For the most part, the questions are versions of, "How does it feel?" and "How difficult is it?" It's like they're interviewing a circus freak. Based on their questions, the professors and students presume that physical disability defines me. There seems to be an expectation for some sophomoric version of a handicapped young man in the music business.

I usually begin with gentle responses to shallow questions, giving them answers like, "It's tough even if you aren't handicapped."

Then in an attempt to encourage questions that are better synch'd with my life, I progress to, "In my career as a musician, I try not to allow my physical disability to enter the equation." In saying this, I'm not dodging reality. I'm attempting to sidetrack questions that beg for a contrived experience or force me to verbalize the obvious and the trite. It never fails that the questions are cliche', presuming a namby pamby mold that I reject.

As the superficial questions proceed, my language and affect become gritty and even aggressive. I tell them, "You kick down the damn door to get what you want." That statement leads to comments like, "You're so strong," triggering a visceral response on my end. I swallow the stomach contents that have leapt up into my throat, take a deep breath, and say, "No, nothing heroic. It's what anyone has to do." I explain that, handicap aside, a musician must be proficient enough to "hang" (hold his or her own) with other musicians. No half-ass performances, handicap or no handicap. I ask the students, "Would you get away with substandard job performance?" Then I tell them, "Other musicians don't take pity on me because I'm in a wheelchair." What shocks me more than anything is that this doesn't seem to have occurred to them. They aren't seeing past cerebral palsy. I hope my irritable responses penetrate their thoughts and cause them to ponder more meaningful inquiries about the life of a musician who pushes the limits against challenging circumstances. I try to stimulate more substantive, insightful questions, but try as I may, in their minds I remain the guy whose disability is his identity.

The university appearances become intolerable for me. Besides, with my level of frustration and aggravation, most of the students probably think of me as a miserable contrarian. There are similarities in TV and radio interviews. They try to talk about my disability as if it frames my career, painting me into a unidimensional existence. Especially during TV and radio dialogues, I try to re-focus the topic on music.

Lively Up Yourself (Bob Marley song)

The phone rings and it's Dick Spratt, longtime family friend and a teacher at Grosse Ile High School. "Dan, I need your help. I'm calling on behalf of the student council. The senior prom is coming up, and the band they chose has cancelled because they double booked. Any chance you could pull something together for us on short notice?" I make some calls. The quintet that I assemble is made up of Detroit session *cats. We won't get to a chance practice, and Bob Marley tunes are hot (1981), so I decide Marley and reggae will be the musical flavor of the event with this group who can pull it off so well.

We show up, me in a wheelchair and beautiful Black musicians, a couple of them in long dreads and African garb. Suddenly, ugly reality crashes down. Here we are at an uppity, all-White school surrounded by a bunch of stuffed-shirt squares. What was I thinking? The scene quickly becomes uptight for all of us when, pointing out one of the school chaperones, the roadie tells me, "That guy just asked me, 'Are they all retarded or just the one in the wheelchair?' I told the asshole that the guy in the wheelchair put this ensemble together and the musicians are world class." Being professionals, we ignore the hateful ignorance and take the stage for the performance.

There's some initial dissatisfaction because the quintet won't be performing a conventional prom play list containing popular pop and rock numbers, and we also won't take requests. We give them Marley hits like "I Shot the Sheriff" and tunes from the

Exodus album. Overall, the music goes over well with high school kids who receive a unique prom experience provided on short notice by Detroit music blue bloods.

Dick Spratt later contacts me to apologize for the attitude and atmosphere among the adults, and I tell him, "We didn't serve it up the way they wanted it." What we actually served was too gourmet for the nouveau riche crowd on Grosse Ile. I realize that event bands provide what is needed and expected, but this was a thrown-together band that provided one hot performance without a rehearsal. As for the ignorant discrimination and elitism we encountered, it's not that I wasn't aware of the social landscape before this incident, but it did make my eyes and ears more acutely aware. The musicians showed class and grace. To this day, there's a bad taste in my mouth when it comes to snooty, pretentious people.

Unsolicited Help

One of the most humiliating incidents of my career takes place in 1984 while I'm performing with a mock southern rock group, Honey Boy, at The Loading Zone, a downriver Detroit bar. When I play congas, I'm in the zone, concentrating fully on the music. I'm trying to ignore the woman who has stepped behind me, but she begins talking into my ear. "I love your face. Instead of staring down at your instrument, you should be looking out at the audience." Annoying jive from an inebriated, self-appointed performance coach! I continue playing—even with her breathing down my neck—until she grasps my hair and pulls my head upward. It's difficult to ignore her now! She apparently believes I'm either deaf or that I'm dismissing her uplifting, confidence-building instructions (which I am!), so she turns up her volume, yelling at me. "Believe you're good looking because you are!"

At this point, Peewee, the guitar player, shouts at her, "Get out of here!" but the band and I continue to play. Following Peewee's stern directive, she returns to the dance floor but keeps her eyes on me. Even after Peewee's rebuke, she returns to her coaching spot behind me several times, repeating her instructions which become even louder demands. Finally, the bouncer escorts her out of the bar. But does she leave the premises? No, she keeps re-entering, and the police are called to manage the situation.

Needless to say, my groove has been broken by a wackadoo who seems to believe she can help me reach some imagined performance potential. Does she think I look down when I'm playing congas because I'm ashamed of my looks? Does she think she can get away with this because I'm at a physical disadvantage? Is she totally unaware of what is acceptable behavior or is she too drunk to care? When you play large venues, there's security and a buffer zone between you and the crowd, but when you play small clubs, there's no barrier and anything can happen.

More Unsolicited Help

I'm at dinner with keyboardist Bernie Worrell who just did a 1984 performance with Talking Heads at Pine Knob. We're eating in a private room at the hotel, and I'm sitting beside David Byrne. We're into a stimulating conversation that began with David's fascination with world music and has progressed to tribal percussion origins in Africa where rhythms are used for ceremonial purposes as well as communication between villages. The topic extends to Afro-Cuban percussion, how its rhythms evoke imagery and spirituality and have been used in *Santeria, a pantheistic religion that incorporates elements of Catholicism. We share observations about Western culture, particularly American immigrant culture, and how it has come to include ancient rhythms in hybrid forms. This leads to the topic of Screamin' Jay Hawkins and his song "I Put a Spell on You."

Out of nowhere a woman approaches, telling me about her brother who is developmentally challenged. She's messing with our vibe, apparently thinking I'm in need of her kind support. Before I know it, she's telling me that I can be healed and rise up out of my wheelchair. She's not only on the wrong track with someone who long ago came to terms with his condition and doesn't welcome her advice, but she's also monopolizing my time during an evening that I'm trying to enjoy. I'll probably never get the chance to talk to David Byrne again! Thankfully, David and Bernie tell her in so many words to get lost, one of them saying, "We're talking business. That's why we reserved this room. Who are you, anyway?" As she turns and leaves, David says, "What is this? Nashville Fan Fair?" He shrugs and tells me, "Look, Dan, I'm sorry. I frequently have to draw lines with people who want something even if it's just attention. They'll go about it under any pretense. They have to be considered a manageable disease. This stuff often comes with dinner." A line has been drawn, no need to tolerate an intrusion in the interest of being polite. We get back to a delightful evening and the conversation we were having before the healer wannabe, or whatever she wanted to be, swooped in.

The same kind of interruption happened again last night during dinner in Detroit with Alexander Zonjic. It would be generous to say that people who do this are trying to be supportive, but David Byrne is right. It's mostly about them. They inject themselves into situations because they crave attention or need to feel they're doing something kind and wonderful—not at all helpful.

Damaged

As always, I'm just trying to listen to the music this evening in 1985 when a man who has been severely burned enters the lounge. His face is so badly disfigured that people can't help doing a double take as he walks past them. His anguish and anger are reflected in his walk, his glare and his voice as he approaches individuals and asks them to hug him, more of a challenge than a request. He's reaching out for acceptance and expecting revulsion and rejection, a traumatized soul who's using aggressive, desperate behaviors that mean, "I dare you to touch me." He's testing people who aren't intending to be cruel, but their faces and stares reveal their dismay. I'm with Mark Conti this evening. Mark has cerebral palsy, too, but less severe than mine. Both of us hug the guy when he stands before us, and we buy him a drink. He's the Elephant Man, John Merrick, saying, "I am not an animal. I'm a human being." Like me, he has a right to exist, and there's a reason he's here.

I'm reliving the sting of prejudice and intolerance through this writing as I recall the parallel between this incident and the one when my right to exist was challenged (this chapter, section My Right to Exist). It's coincidental that both incidents took place at *Your Mustache.

Singer Out of Synch

*Club Industry, a music venue in Pontiac, Michigan, is packed. *Dan Lewis & Friends is groovin' during a performance in 1990. We're performing the number "Unloved Children" from Todd

Rundgren's album *Nearly Human*. The sections are all coming together, and guitarist Al Ayoub goes out there with a solo echoing Hendrix's "Purple Haze." The room is transformed by heady vibes in this rare moment, energy moving from stage to audience and back again. We're allowing the music to take us higher and higher when suddenly the singer, front and center, raises his hands to indicate that the number is over. The spell is broken.

When you hear music, after it's over, it's gone, in the air.
You can never capture it again.

Eric Dolphy

Like so many singers, ours is just a singer, not a fully immersed musician. He's not hip to the concepts of key or the directions improvisation can take in solos. He's taking the role of front man too literally, treating the rest of the group as if we're his back-ups. Because he doesn't understand what's going on, he thinks the tune has spiraled out of control and intervenes to save the performance. What he has actually done is reel in a beautiful, graceful sailfish in mid-air, believing it needed to be saved it from drowning.

No Jam Session Here

*Dan Lewis and Friends is playing at *Baker's Keyboard Lounge in 1991. We've looked forward to this gig and have rehearsed a jazz-contemporary set that includes "Follow Your Heart" by Joe Farrell and an obscure David Sanborn tune, "Hobbies." The place is packed with people listening, drinking and soaking in the atmosphere.

There's an organ summit happening nearby at the Magic Bag. Three Hammond B-3 organists, Charles Earland, Lyman Woodard and John Patton, stop in to hear us. Charles is an internationally known organist who also plays soprano sax. Taking it for granted that because he's a star he can just walk onto the stage at Baker's and share our performance, Charles begins preparing his horn. I ask him, "Charles, what are you doing?" He replies, "Gonna sit in with you guys." This hits me as presumptuous, and I tell him, "No you're not. I wouldn't do that to you. I've never even met you before. You should ask first. The stage is as sacred a place to me as it is to you. Let's respect that."

The stage at Baker's is well known in the music world, considered by some to be the world's oldest jazz club. Who wouldn't want to perform on this stage? For my band, it's a coveted opportunity in a revered setting. I'm aware that Mr. Baker would probably prefer that I allow this renowned jazz musician to share the stage with us, but I stick to principles that require basic stage etiquette and mutual respect for fellow musicians. Besides, this isn't a jam session. The musicians performing with me rehearsed the sets that we're playing, and the compositions we've chosen aren't standards that will accommodate unrehearsed solos.

At the end of the night, Charles is still sitting at the bar. I approach him and explain that under the circumstances, I felt having an impromptu sit-in wouldn't have done our music justice and also wouldn't have been fair to the other musicians. I tell him that I respect his artistry but that he hadn't rehearsed our sets, adding that my group put their time in rehearsing before we took the stage. It's simple. He didn't know the music. He sincerely was not intending to be an interloper, responding, "I just noticed you have a horn section. You know, saxophone was my first instrument." Lyman and John sit by quietly. I believe they understand my position. Even Itzhak Perlman's violin, played impromptu, could have a negative impact on a symphony.

The Voice Lesson

One evening in 2015 at an off-the-radar downriver nightclub, I'm sitting with Martha Reeves whose brother is sitting in, doing an Al Green tune. We're in an unmarked building, a speakeasy with a sound stage, a pool table and a bar. Acoustically and functionally, it's the equivalent of a Manhattan rehearsal loft, a place to hang out and listen to bands and singer-songwriters as they work on their originals. Sometimes their work morphs into jam sessions of multi-genre cover tunes.

Over the years, my voice has become more and more muted and harsh. Martha says to me, "You're struggling with your voice, aren't you?" I respond, "Yes. My projection is getting weaker as I get older. Even on a good day it sounds like I gargled with razor blades." She tells me, "There are voice exercises that will open up your airways. If you breathe deeply, you won't have to depend on your throat. Trust me. I know it works, but the results will come over time." I'm thinking, "Wow, I'll bet she's had some great voice coaches." She offers to show me here and now. I ask, "Are you sure?" She says, "Yes. Let's get started" and begins coaching me on breathing. Right here in a nightclub, Martha shows me exercises to strengthen my voice. They involve using the diaphragm and expanding the lungs rather than just speaking with the throat. As we do the exercise together, I'm having flashbacks of breathing exercises that were taught to me by respiratory therapists. This exercise is challenging, but I swallow my pride, tamp down my self-consciousness and attempt it. I can't help chuckling because I'm sure we're looking ridiculous.

I love broadcasting and would have enjoyed being a disc jockey. What a dream job, spinning records, talking music and interviewing musicians. It might have been possible years ago, even with my scratchy voice, if not for dyslexia. I can't read print copy. The lesson with Martha Reeves triggers memories of wanting to be a DJ with a big voice and the times when Dan Carlisle, a personality on WABX and W4, allowed me to observe while he was on the air. Great memories, but man, Martha, I'm never going to be a singer or a DJ.

Pedantic

Here it is again, my elitist relative scale. I've been guilty of beating intelligent people over the head with fine points that I consider to be important, fine points that in my opinion, are steps on an ascending staircase. Talking to myself rather than out loud, although snarky words have occasionally slid across my tongue, I wonder, "Do you know the difference between smooth jazz and bebop? They're not on the same level whatsoever!" It's a harsh judgment on the unenlightened.

Recently I've taken a softer look through a wider lens and understand that people appreciate all art on their own terms, even those who say "I love jazz" followed by "I love Kenny G," unaware of any artistic gap between the two. Those who don't share my relative value scale are simply choosing their own dessert. How many people enjoy music merely for the sound of it and the emotions it evokes without any consideration of the scales, notes, tempos or arrangements? Music is supposed to be enjoyed. I've been so serious, so entrenched in ideology, that I've limited my own enjoyment while imposing my discernment on others. I need to focus my own audio. Live and let live. I'm working on this.

History Repeats

"You're an asshole! You're taking over." Al Ayoub's voice can take on a hard edge, an edge that comes out when I push the envelope, this time with a behavior I've repeated many times over the years. It's a reflex with me. Wouldn't you think I'd learn to pause, take a breath and go with the flow?

In this case, Al is running an idea past me, not extending an invitation for me to reinvent his vision. Instead of just going with his practical concept of a small Jimi Hendrix tribute band, I jump into go-big-or-go-home mode, proposing a ten-piece group and symphonic arrangements that fuse Hendrix, Gil Evans and Miles Davis. It's like Al has asked me over for pizza, and I'm demanding for a four-course meal. He never stays mad at me for very long, but I've probably succeeded in killing this project. I got so excited about the prospects that I jumped ahead of the project—wanting to do things in a BIG way. At the same time, I realize that the big band concept is cost prohibitive and can put your own finances at risk. Right-sizing can be effective and beautiful. Al has done it.

My expectations and demands for BIG are longstanding—BIG sound, BIG number of musicians, BIG because I need BIG. I've pondered the psychology of my need for performance blowouts. Trumpeter Lew Soloff (Blood, Sweat & Tears) was responsive, willing, and gracious when I contacted him in 2003 about the prospect of performing with *Dan Lewis & Friends at the NorEast'r, a fledgling music and arts festival in a remote area of northern Michigan. As it turned out, the festival's board of directors decided to schedule Richie Havens instead because they felt he was a good fit with their folkish audience. The other reason was that the Dan Lewis & Friends with Lew Soloff concept was growing into a BIG group of musicians at a BIG cost, more than the small nonprofit could afford. This left me to call Lew and thank him for his willingness. Looking back now, I can see that I was adhering to my usual modus operandi, go big or go home.

I can't seem to shake it and have repeated this tendency as recently as 2019. It's the devil that sits on my left shoulder, whispering in my ear. It's the reason I would never find satisfaction in a bar band. I need big and perfect to the point that I get in my own way. Edgar Winter mentioned my relentless pursuit of perfection, and so did Al Jarreau. If it lacks size, luster and perfection, it's not for me. I'm always trying to construct a magnificent tower because of my own insecurities.

CHAPTER TEN
Blind Alleys

I'm half man and half horse 'cause there's a
lot of shit in the streets.

Dan Lewis

Barricades have never deterred me from taking resolute walks to the record store, metaphorically speaking. Am I an optimist or a fool? Tenacity, perseverance and steadfast focus are traits that have been encouraged and nurtured by musician brothers who on the one hand have taken the time and effort to include me but on the other hand have cut me little slack. The result is a Dan Lewis who aims high when it comes to music and who is determined when it comes to how to proceed in life. This chapter contains visions, dreams and desires that turned into disappointments, regrets and lessons learned.

A Long Walk in MacArthur Park (MacArthur Park is a song by Jimmy Webb)

To begin at the end of a long history that begins in the mid-1960s, Jimmy Webb has not merely fallen off the pedestal that he occupied in my heart and mind for a very long time. He leapt.

Having followed Jimmy's career for nearly fifty years, there are few music historians who know as much about his life and work as I do. For years, an interview with him has been on the list of things I want to do. I've compiled a comprehensive set of questions, thoughtfully composed to provide a detailed and intimate documentary of his life and compositions. The topics cover periods of his life and aspects of his career that only a serious Webb devotee would know. This fact alone would make the interview really his, including details about the man and his music that bring his story to life, not a cursory, boring or shallow look inside his career.

Because I've attended so many of his live performances, Jimmy recognizes me immediately in a receiving line. At The Ark in Ann Arbor, Michigan, I ask him for the interview, and he warmly tells me, "For you, we'll make it happen. Maybe we could do it with me at the piano, and we'll have a good time doing it, too." This puts me over the moon, but I'm not so giddy with excitement that I'm unrealistic. I ask him, "Are you sure you'll have time to do this with your new book (*The Cake and the Rain: A Memoir*, 2017) coming out?" He responds, "We'll get it done."

In the meantime, I contact Laura Savini, his manager wife, and offer to do the interview at his convenience. I tell her that I will meet him on location during a tour if that would be easiest for him. Still feeling confident months later, I'm in a receiving line after his performance at the Macomb Center for the Performing Arts. I hand him the draft of potential interview questions, which have also been sent via email, along with my contact information. He accepts the envelope, but this time he tells me half-heartedly, "Perhaps we can do this by phone." At this moment, I can sense that he has no intention of doing the interview. To date, there's been no response.

Here's a scenario that speaks volumes. I'm in a post-performance receiving line at the Kirtland Center for the Performing Arts (Grayling, Michigan) accompanied by Al Ayoub who is a guitarist with the Detroit Symphony Orchestra. Upon hearing that Al performs with the DSO, Jimmy's interest is piqued. He expresses a desire to perform with the DSO, and it's immediately apparent that my request for an interview is nothing more than a nuisance. During this encounter, he looks at me with a dubious smile, as if he's looking at a lower life form, and refers to me as a Webb Head. The moniker reduces me to groupie status, but it also reflects his insensitivity. It's apparent that he's totally focused on self and trying to avoid expending time and energy on an exercise that might not benefit his career. After all, I'm not affiliated with a publication, and I'm not a well known journalist or documentarian.

Finally in 2017, I acknowledge reality. Jimmy's interactions with me have been a *riff, and like a fool I've been *comping, partly in a quest for the interview and partly because I can't bear to admit that he doesn't stand atop the pedestal where I've placed him since I was seven years old. It's a traumatic discovery that Jimmy's personal attributes don't match his creative genius. So much for my glorified image of him. The truth is that some great songwriters do it as a craft and do it masterfully, but the essence of their art doesn't necessarily reside as deeply within them as you had imagined.

I'm a music historian. Before I get involved in a project, I do my homework. In Jimmy Webb's case, it was done over five decades, and I know without a doubt that I could have done a stellar interview. Well, Jimmy, I wanted to bake you a cake, but you left me out in the rain holding the batter.

Entrance (album by Edgar Winter)

Edgar Winter and I meet in 1972 in Fort Lauderdale, Florida through a mutual friend, Leslie West. Edgar's band White Trash, his spin on a Ray Charles big band made up of White cats playing R&B originals and some covers, opens at a Mountain concert featuring Leslie. White Trash knocks me on my ass!

Edgar is making his money playing rock 'n roll, but there's so much more to his work. *Entrance* is beautiful, an album of serious music released in 1970, his first recording with Columbia Records. I love *Entrance* because of its introspection and the way it comes full circle in self-discovery. It's a journey upward in songs that are woven together with emotions. I can imagine it as a neo-symphonic arrangement performed by classical *cats. To get some face time with Edgar and propose a project I'm envisioning, I catch up with him at a Scientology convention in Los Angeles. I share my idea without any commitment on his end, and it's left up to me to get back with him when the plan is more solid.

After a few years of contact with Edgar's wife, Monique, who is positive about my vision, a dinner meeting in New York City is arranged to explore the possibility of a live, symphonic version of *Entrance*. Edgar still doesn't commit, merely saying that if it works, we'd start small and expand later, adding that he'll let me know how much money he'd need to do it. At this point, he has The Edgar Winter Group and is also recording on other artists' albums. Monique tells me that Edgar's management wants him to continue playing the hits, cash cows for them. Her reservation is that he's not known for the type of music I'm proposing. She says,

"How can we know if the artistic crowd will even take to it?" At one point, she tells me, "We would have to do it without management." I'm excited that Edgar and Monique might consider working directly with me. Getting to this point has been achieved with the support and guidance of Mel Ball, a Detroit booking agent who is helping me bring the project together clearly on paper.

I want this so badly that I've offered to put up the money, realizing the risk involved. It would include Joe LoDuca's jazz fusion rhythm section. I'm driven by the dream of a successful remake, half *Entrance* and half deep cuts of some of Edgar's pieces that weren't hits, followed by an *Entrance* tour. Prior to obtaining his agreement, the stage is being set in advance by getting the Birmingham-Bloomfield Symphony Orchestra and conductor Felix Resnick on board as well as discussing the writing of charts for symphonic arrangements. On a trip to L.A., I'm introduced to the Synclavier, a digital synthesizer that could expand our abilities and efficiency in developing charts. This could be nirvana, the perfection I'm obsessed with, and I tell Edgar about it. It would take time to acquire and implement, but it would save time in the long run, a technological tool to advance this project.

I arrive at a dinner meeting with Edgar in New York City accompanied by two friends, both musicians. Whether they intend to or not, my sidekicks monopolize the conversation and sidetrack my agenda. Egos and ambitions have a way of strutting about in the presence of someone who is famous. Time is wasted, and the purpose of my long awaited face-to-face with Edgar is undermined. I'm pissed. It's a business lesson that I take to heart. On the flight home, I'm resolutely thinking, "I've got this. It's going to work." Hip to what happened at our meeting, Edgar later tells me,

"I thought it was supposed to be about your vision. If it's yours, don't let other people steal your thunder. They'll try." Noted. I continue to pursue the vision.

The problem with this entire scene is that I'm chasing Edgar around the country to pitch the project to him in person. One night I go alone in a cab to *Harpos in Detroit, giving no thought to the dangerous neighborhood or how I'd get back home. I deliver the project tapes to Edgar after his performance. At 3:00 a.m., I wheel myself into an alley amidst snarling German shepherds to get to a street where I think there might be a chance of flagging down a taxi. But...it could be a while before one passes by...if at all. I'm thinking I'll die here, killed by vicious dogs that will chew on my corpse. When I make it to the street, good luck is with me and a cab soon happens by. The driver stops, picks me up and says, "What the hell are you doing here at this hour?" He takes me all the way to my door.

I'll never forget the night in 1984 when Edgar called with his decision. "Dan, I won't be able to do this." He explains that the project isn't going to happen because of another offer, a Leon Russell tour attached to a five-year contract with a dual billing— Leon Russell and Edgar Winter. I'm literally sick hearing this and can feel my stomach beginning to spasm. I ask him, "Can you hold on?" He says, "Sure, Dan." He holds on as I compose myself. An *Entrance* tour, my ultimate dream, is dead. I've never wanted anything so much, not only for him but for myself, performing with Edgar Winter. He says several times how sorry he is that it didn't work out.

Edgar was gracious and honest. I know making that call to me was difficult. Even though he had said he'd love to do the project if we could make it work, he ultimately made a decision based on what would provide reliable money. I didn't talk to Edgar again for several years, not because of any hard feelings but because of my deep disappointment after pursuing a project for so long. He has now been a friend for forty-seven years, and I'm indebted to him for helping me remove music industry blinders. I've learned that commercial endeavors often win out over artistic visions. Reality can be painful. Until a deal is closed, it's not a done deal.

Horizon: An Experiment

My mission in putting together a band called Horizon in 1976 is to maximize flexibility and expand the delivery of diverse sounds using an operational concept called jobbing, floating musicians from various other groups in and out of a band as needed and as available. Jazz musicians dig jobbing because it keeps them working and provides a constantly changing music landscape. For me, it also keeps the mind open and teaches one to never rule anything out. To be locked into a fixed group's way of doing things is to cheat yourself. I'm thinking it isn't necessary to have a constant set of musicians in a group for every performance. Jobbing isn't fickle, unstable or about ownership, but some of the rock guys respond with, "You're stealing my bass player!"

I rent the Trenton Theater and stage a show there. Horizon only plays one concert, but it's a sold out performance! My experiment demonstrates that rock 'n roll musicians are less adaptable to floating in and out of groups. For something like this to succeed, everyone has to work off the same page, and the musicians involved have to buy into the jobbing concept. Beyond the operational mismatch, working with this group of rock musicians highlights differences in performance potential. Many rock musicians don't read music. They lift tunes from records and play them rote. Inability to read music limits performance potential, particularly if one strives to improvise. This is why rock musicians and other contemporary musicians, the ones who have vision and can afford it, hire jazz *cats to open up and enhance an arrangement.

Years later in the '90s, jobbing is successfully operationalized with jazz musicians in *Dan Lewis and Friends. Further affirmation of what the ability to read music adds comes in 1993 when singer-songwriter Dan Hall and I play at a globally televised performance for Catholic religious leaders at a liturgical conference in Cleveland. There's a large symphony and a conductor, and all the musicians are astute readers who follow what is on the page. I keep my eyes on the baton, open my ears to every instrument and each part in the symphony, and concentrate on delivering my part within the greater context.

Elusive Butterfly

"Dan, I'm working with Bryan [Ferry] on a solo album, and he's looking for Ornette Coleman. I told him if anyone can find him, Dan Lewis can." It's drummer Andy Newmark. Ornette is legendary, a sought after but elusive saxophonist, the king of avant-garde saxophone.

> **Jazz is the only music in which the same notes can be played night after night, but differently each time.**
> **Ornette Coleman**

Having accompanied Andy to eight cities on Bryan's solo tour two years ago (1986), I'm grateful for that experience. Bryan allowed me to attend post-performance critiques with the band.

He's pure British class, gallant, an aristocrat. I'd like to help him find Ornette if I can.

Forever driving into the same rut in the road in pursuit of a holy grail, I'm operating under an impression that money won't be an issue. Hoping for something more solid than an impression, I make a call to Andy just to be sure they're on a serious quest to find this enigmatic *cat. "If I find Ornette, are you sure he'll be used?" The reply: "Yes. His signature style is needed for several tunes on the album." I make calls and connections, even calling Paris, France. Ornette's son Denardo is his manager in New York City, so I make calls to friends there to locate him. I explain that yes, Bryan really wants Ornette and that I wouldn't go to so much trouble for just anyone. Bryan Ferry isn't just anyone. Long story short, after many somersaults, they track Denardo down and I make contact, but the deal doesn't go down because Ornette's price is prohibitive.

I'm disappointed because I was hoping I could help Bryan get Ornette's sound on the album. In this business, there are many elusive butterflies. You shouldn't get excited or think they're in the jar before the lid is tightened.

The Dangling Project

I'm reading the newspaper at a friend's house in Los Angeles in 1993. "Damn! Bennie Maupin is playing at the Vine Street Bar & Grill. We've got to go hear him!"

The performance brings back what I'd heard Herbie Hancock's Headhunters deliver years ago, and I'm reminded how much Bennie influenced that great music. He still has the magic touch that made those records great in the '70s. I wave Bennie over to our table and introduce myself as a fellow Detroiter. "You became a soundtrack in my life when you recorded with Herbie Hancock." As I talk with him, I ask what he'd think of recording his progressive bebop compositions, and he says, "Yes, I'd love that." It's agreed that Bennie will come to Detroit to work with me on the project.

In preparation, I start looking for home run session *cats. I contact Jim Beard (Steely Dan) in New York City. He provides solid advice and recommends musicians. He would make a great producer for this project, but during input from others, I allow my preferences and ultimately my vision to get diluted. There's compromise on choice of musicians. I really want to capture the interplay and camaraderie between Bennie Maupin (saxophone, flute, clarinet) and Eddie Henderson (trumpet), but I can't afford both of them. I end up with great Detroit musicians. To save money, there's no producer. I've been advised to use a studio in New York City, but instead I get drawn into what is touted as the latest and greatest sound gear in the greater Detroit area. There's a studio where Pro Tools, a fairly new studio outboard technology, is available. I check out the credentials of the owner-engineer and give him the job. When the recording portion of the project is finished, Bennie tells me, "I'm going to leave the rest to you, Dan. I'll be back in a couple of weeks."

The end result is that the Detroit musicians are fine, but the technology and engineering are not. Slow computers result in bleeding of instruments into each other without isolation of each one, causing an impure, adulterated sound. The engineer not only hasn't mastered the technology, but he also lacks experience with a full-scale album project. For months, he re-engineers and adjusts. A musician friend lends technical assistance, but talented musicians don't necessarily have the skills of a sound engineer. I'm frustrated and dissatisfied with the quality of the mixes except for three tunes that are pretty good—not to mention the entire project is subject to my stinkin' thinkin'. Everything must be perfect.

During this fiasco, I go to a Rickie Lee Jones concert at The Ark, a music venue in Ann Arbor, Michigan, and I sit at a table in the front row. My thoughts are jumbled with frustration and disappointment. Rickie visits my table after her performance. My mental and emotional state must be apparent because she says, "You look like you're deep in thought. Are you unhappy? Didn't you like my set?" I tell her about the Maupin project gone awry, my deepest concern being that I've let Bennie down. Rickie is empathetic, at one point telling me, "Stop right there. You haven't failed. You got sidetracked. Allow yourself to believe you've accomplished something." During our brief conversation, she also tells me, "You need to stick to your own vision. Shut out the noise and interference. Don't let others own it. You own it." Uh huh, sound familiar, Dan?

During the extended period of time when the sound quality is being fixed, it's never good enough for me. I'd promised to get the project done quickly, but time drags on. The engineer doesn't seem to take responsibility for the poor quality. I'm angry at myself for listening to too many others, everyone except the ones I should have listened to. I'm under great pressure and embarrassed. Bennie, pissed and disappointed, still wants to get the recording released. When some tracks go missing, Bobby Lewis, who had advised me not to do the recording sessions where they were done, is tempted to say, "I told you so." Ultimately, the Maupin recording never sees the light of day.

For a long time, I feel that this unfinished project has put a strain on my relationship with Bennie. He's a kind person, patient and understanding. I should have had tighter control, but I allowed others too much input rather than sticking to my initial plan. Roughly 18 years later (2011), Bennie and I consider another attempt. I call Felix Cavaliere (The Rascals), a singer-producer in New York City, for guidance. After giving him a short narrative of the project, he tells me, "I wouldn't touch it. You aren't going to be satisfied no matter what. Don't put any more money into it." There it is! Felix recognizes straight away, as I have no doubt Bennie does, that a quest for perfection is one of the primary causes of the project never reaching completion.

Looking back now, it's clear that the project failed because I didn't follow my own instincts and allowed my demand for perfection to get in the way. I should have gone with my initial desire to work with Jim Beard. It would have taken less time at lower cost in the end. Expenses piled up over two or three years. I knew at the time that artists who were getting bookings were using CDs as calling cards. On that landscape, I believed this recording had to be as close to flawless as possible, especially the work of Bennie Maupin. What happened then won't happen again. I take responsibility for the failure of the project, but it has hardened me.

Mirages

To repeat what I said at the beginning of this chapter, barricades have never deterred me from taking resolute walks to the record store. I prepare painstakingly prior to auditions for well known artists only to realize later that it was all for naught. I often wonder, after working so hard, why it doesn't pay off. In my case, it's cerebral palsy and dyslexia. Because of it, hard work and determination don't guarantee success in these situations.

I've been nurtured and encouraged by music masters who've taught me that my handicap shouldn't get in the way when it comes to musicianship—and it hasn't. During auditions, you're being checked out closely including your real-time reactions within a dynamic piece. They can add wrinkles like changing it up without notice to see if you can adapt quickly and keep it seamless. They need to have someone who isn't tripped up by unexpected changes in an arrangement. Do you panic? Do you listen to and fit in with the entire ensemble or are you merely focusing on your part? They might even ask you to play tunes that you didn't rehearse. What you think will go down during an audition might not. I'm good with tempos, but the importance of the ability to read music can't be under-stated. This puts me at a disadvantage.

I'm glad I had these experiences even though I didn't land the gigs. As much as I hate to pull the handicap card, a guy in a wheelchair is a complication that others don't want to deal with, especially when the job involves life on the road. In all fairness, if they didn't consider my physical state a complication, knowing the rigors of touring, they'd be operating from behind blinders. I'm stuck in place unless I hitch this wheelchair to the back bumper of a tour bus.

CHAPTER ELEVEN
My Vinyl Temple

**My music is the spiritual expression of what I am...
my faith, my knowledge, my being.**

John Coltrane

There was some debate about whether the contents of this chapter, some of it stream of consciousness, belong in this book. Our conclusion was that they're foundational to who I am, as much a part of my story as the music, people, places and happenings herein. Without question, my circumstances and experiences have shaped my beliefs, so they can't be separated.

**If you take the creation of music and the creation of your own life
values as your overall goal, then living becomes a musical process.**

Cecil Taylor

♫

I was merely looking at a Byrds album cover or taking in a track that Miles was layin' down, unaware that I was stepping into a life-long religion. For me, there was no defining moment or epiphany involved, no rebirth through baptism or being "saved," just as there's no conscious awareness that your hormones are changing as you approach adolescence. Music and faith are one and the same in my heart and mind. It's about hunger and thirst and therefore not a conscious choice.

The concept of mortality was conjured up in my brain by a Traffic song, "No Time to Live." It's about a suicidal guy and uses a set of jazz chords that transported me, causing me to consider my own mortality and the possibility that life and death exist on a metaphysical grid. Initially, I didn't have words for the concept, and alternative esoteric angles caused trouble for me at school. When I chose the topic for a report and questioned the widely held belief in human existence on a unidimensional plane, it resulted in stern inquiries and challenges from thought police who took me to task. Perhaps they felt a need to pull me back from nihilism or a spiritual abyss. I was basically told, "How dare you." I'd hit one more jagged guard rail in the school setting. I talked to my mom about it. She knew I was just a kid trying to wrap his head around the human condition.

I'm a believer in the other side. My soul will live beyond this flesh-bound existence, and there are many kindred souls and sweet vibrations waiting for all of us. I have a fascination with death and the dimension beyond, but it's not a death wish. I don't buy into God fearing or fear of death and gravitate toward a balance between realism and what some would call mysticism, the latter often spoken of as if it's an opposing belief or less valid than Christianity and its various denominations.

Too often organized religions rail against each other using simplistic us-versus-them thinking as if it's a football game. My parents didn't attend church, and it's just as well. Within a church or denomination, good people can come together and do great things for others, but so far on a global scale there's been as much damage and destruction as there has been unity, comfort and mercy in the name of a god. What I've noticed about organized religion is that it's too often made up of people enjoying their own pain and trying to control others through fear and guilt. They don't take responsibility for what happens around them because it's "God's will." I tend to think of staunch churchgoers in terms of their psychological frailty. The rub occurs when they undertake a mission to shepherd fellow human beings toward the Lord and salvation. People try to get you to accept a certain way of thinking, but the packaged doctrines don't resonate with me. I don't hand personal power over to a higher power or man-made religions, and I don't throw money into church collection plates. I realize people find solace in church, but too many religious leaders cash in on the herd mentality.

Then there are the sexist practices that have historically been part and parcel of religion with give and take from social and cultural roots. The men's group at a former girlfriend's church recommends that men not share their innermost feelings with their spouses because women expect men to be towers of strength who will shield them from harsh realities and take care of them. How insulting to women! My take on that dialogue is that these church men believe they're the stronger gender, a perspective caused by testosterone poisoning and a narrow cultural perspective. In my experience, women are the stronger gender physically and emotionally. I don't admire men who never show weakness or vulnerability. I'm off on a tangent triggered by an experience at a church, but I do struggle with the behavior of any man who feels the need to maintain a macho image or is convinced that he's the sole head of a household. Paternalism and male dominance—the source of so much that's wrong in the world. It's hard to believe this topic is still relevant.

Like those who are on a mission save souls, sometimes I think I can help others because of an assumption on my part that they want to evolve...an uppity, self-serving and self-defeating premise. Evolve to what? To my way of looking at life and the hereafter? What gives me the audacity to think I can or should? My ego? I need to straighten my own self out. And not only that, the role of shaman and therapist drains me, and ultimately nothing changes. This type of quest is as misguided as others' well intended shepherding and their desire to heal my physical condition through faith (Chapter 12: Mama Said There'd Be Days Like This, section An Altar Named Reality).

Life in this flesh-bound dimension isn't easy for anyone. I believe my existence will get easier someday even through death. I'm not having a romance with death, but I don't fear it, either. There are a number of written works and philosophers whose perspectives give me strength and cause to ponder. I appreciate the writings of Christopher Hitchens, Gore Vidal and William Blake. They've enhanced my coping and bolstered my sanity, such as it is. On that note, I find the ranting, suicidal news anchor Howard Beale in the film *Network* fascinating.

When asked if I belong to a particular religion, I say, "Yes, all of them." At the same time, I'm thinking, "They all believe what they all believe." I acknowledge the positive universals in religious doctrines (do unto others..., love thy neighbor...) and the good work that churches do. For as long as I can remember, I've been comforted by a life force, a spiritual presence that surrounds all of us, but it's larger than the boundaries of religion. Beyond that awareness, music nurtures me and gives me strength when all else fails.

Early 1970s: Looking Eastward

Indian ragas are classical music with ancient roots. They sound simple but are actually quite complicated, having a rhythmic pulse that focuses on mood, emotion exploration and capturing seasons and colors. They use the same pentatonic scale as Western music but apply it differently. This attracted the interest of jazz musicians in the 1940s and '50s because of the improvisational possibilities. I've been enamored of ragas since first hearing sitar maestro Ravi Shankar when he was introduced to the Western world by George Harrison.

It strikes me that Eastern music and those who perform it, such as the tabla (Indian drum) musician Alla Rakha, do so from a place of self-discovery and transcendence—perfect for a man who uses imagination and daydreaming to escape his body. I've no interest in being on the ground, so I dream of flying higher and ever higher, crescendoing to a spiritual place. It's not that a feet-on-the-ground perspective isn't necessary in most life circumstances, but I also want to travel outside this body, knowing that I must return to earth for the time being.

I'm unable to get into the yoga positions, so I've tried droning. It's done with a machine that draws out a metered tone, slow and wide, a singular note that gradually increases in volume. It's relaxing and pheromones are released. Like Eastern music, droning is a vehicle that allows me to travel.

1976-1978: Music and Mysticism

'76 is a dark time in my life. My physical state is inescapable, so I'm searching for a detour around it that will allow me to pursue what I need more than anything—to study and perform percussion—but that's putting it mildly. I must. I'm driven. It's a spiritual hunger.

*Cobb's Corner at Cass Avenue and Willis Street provides a venue for great jazz where I catch a set by Griot Galaxy (avant-garde jazz) with drummer-composer Ali Mora, a.k.a. Francisco Mora. I'm looking for a percussion teacher. If one believes, as I do, that everything happens for a reason, fate has led me to Ali who in turn introduces me to Larry Fratangelo, percussionist in the band Cordova. Larry becomes my teacher and steadfast comrade through many adventures, memorable experiences, good times and hard times.

While the universe is aligning with my needs, Ali bestows upon me a much needed gift in the form of *Nam Myōhō Renge Kyō*, Buddhist chanting used to prepare the mind for meditation. It calms my anxiety and heightens my perceptions, releasing tension and improving my life condition. I think of it as morphing the molecules (Chapter 14). As I move deeper, or more aptly higher, into Buddhist chanting, I experience how the energy increases with the number of chanting people. Chanting helps me trust and believe in myself. It allows me to be present in the moment and leads me to empathy. It also improves my self-acceptance and healthy ego development. It serves me well for a year until I begin to feel pressure to recruit others and spread the message. In this respect, it's akin to Christian missionary efforts. Anything that smells like herd mentality creates a barrier for me.

1978: Alice

Creative and artistic endeavors have a mission that goes far beyond just making music for the sake of music.

Herbie Hancock

She allows me to occupy a special place with her for a brief time over a shared dish of brown rice after her performance in Recital Hall at the Detroit Institute of Arts. She's strikingly thin and frail, perhaps due to hours spent in prayer, strict adherence to a Hindu diet and because she needs little food. Music and spirituality sustain her. There's a beautiful aura surrounding her, not a trace of ego. She exudes peace and kindness. It strikes me that her compositions reflect these qualities.

Alice McLeod Coltrane, native Detroiter and wife of the late jazz legend John Coltrane. I've met her through my friend, percussionist Roy Brooks. Today's performance featured Alice on piano and Hammond organ, Roy on drums and Reggie Workman on acoustic bass. Like John's, Alice's improvisation is lengthy. She allows the musicians to express themselves, no time limits. Sharing this simple meal with her causes a light to switch on in my brain. It's as if her simple diet and inner peace inform her music, her chord progressions and the way she travels outside herself. Her music and her spirituality are one and the same. Spiritual strength inspires her music and together they sustain her.

When I say Alice allows me to share a special place with her, it's based not only on the aura that surrounds her but also the enlightening conversation. "Self-discipline allows you to become one with your craft, as a part of everything else, to reach the highest human level." As I'm trying to wrap my brain around this intersection of music, food, faith and life, she continues, "John lost some people later in his life, but it was more important to allow the spiritual to inform his music." She also tells me, in so many words, that her compositions are musical prayers. Alice composes and performs jazz, but her overarching dedication is to Eastern philosophy, more specifically Buddhism.

As I'm struggling with profound disappointment over my inability to use a full drum set, compounded by an inability to play tablas because of my fingers, these brief but impactful moments with Alice Coltrane touch me on a deep level. Tranquility and acceptance of my limitations, along with hope for yet unforeseen prospects, wash over me. Thank you, Alice. Spiritual calm, reality and life's possibilities merge.

Lessons

There's purity in the acceptance of others. Acceptance and respect are required even if I reject an ideology. It requires that I reserve dislikes, comparisons and judgments, sitting suspended at the intersection of reality and spirituality. I try to consider the perspective of the person/persons I'm relating to, realizing that each has his/her own perspective on the way things are or the way things should be. If we agree about something, it's a bonus.

There's a oneness in Eastern religion and philosophy that I think of as open humanism, building on the positive aspects of people and calling forth the best in them or at least what is needed for the moment, for the project, or for life. There's beauty in common ground. Each person brings something different to a project, a situation or a piece of music. Relying on their own strengths and creativity, human beings can evolve naturally, elevating self and humanity. It reminds me of Alice Coltrane's no-limits approach to jazz improvisation for herself and musicians who played with her and how Miles Davis allowed each musician to discover his or her own artistry without any "my way" or how-to instructions. I think of it as artful coming together, and it has everything to do with faith and religion.

Having a longstanding desire to navigate the unknown and even more so to acquire a deeper understanding of consciousness and perpetuity, I'm pondering an ancient concept known as the Akashic Chronicle, an energy field believed to hold a compendium of all thoughts, words, emotions and even intent. It's a living cyclorama of past, present and future without linear time. It's intriguing that one might experience all human events simultaneously on an ethereal plane. Could it be the peaceful, joyous non-place where all consciousness resides? Does this conflict with the Christian belief in a heaven or the belief in afterlife of other religions? I think not. Do we return here to a flesh-bound cycle to complete unfinished evolution? We're all becoming, awakening as we move toward metaphysical elevation. We're second density beings (consciousness exploring what it's like to be organic), and each scene is a rehearsal.

CHAPTER TWELVE
Mama Said There'd Be Days Like This*

*Danny, there will never be a woman who can
compete with your music including me. You'll never
love a woman as much as you love music.*

Suzanne Lewis, Dan's mother

Narrative by Leonard King, Jr.

There's no other person on planet Earth who has the same IDENTICAL personality as Danny Lewis. I've traveled throughout all of the industrial nations, and although I honestly can't claim to have met everyone throughout this huge global geography, I've yet to meet anyone quite like him. However, if Danny has a twin personality out there, I want to meet this person—right now.

---

* Song written by Luther Dixon and Willie Denson, recorded by The Shirelles

We met during the American bicentennial year of 1976. At the time, I was hosting a radio program on WDET-FM Detroit titled "Full Circle" which was broadcast every Monday evening for 5 1/2 years. It was also during that year I used to request that Detroit area musicians send me copies of their works on vinyl, cassette, or reel-to-reel tapes as a way for me to promote them on my program—alerting the public to the fact that there were artists out there worthy of being heard and whose works did not have an outlet via commercial radio. Danny sent me a tape of a performance his group recorded at the Trenton Theater. We met when he came to one of my gigs somewhere later in '76. That was when I found out he was born with cerebral palsy and was confined to a wheelchair, but there wasn't anything limited about his demeanor and his energy as I watched him interact with his friends. For example, he wanted to go somewhere specifically, but one of his friends was trying to convince him to do something else instead. Danny looked at the guy and said, "No, no, no, no, no—that's not what I wanna do." He made it perfectly clear that he wasn't going to be manhandled by anyone just because he had to sit in that wheelchair. Others may have viewed him as handicapped but he had the audacity to get what he wanted and go where he wanted to go which was a testament to his overall determination. I hired Danny to play conga drums and percussion in my band many times during the 1980s. Given the physicality of his hands (due to the palsy), I wasn't concerned about him playing conga drums like Mongo Santamaria or Ray Barretto. What he had was genuine enough to fit in with all the music my group was playing at the time.

There was one rehearsal at my home in 1986 when I threatened to put Danny out of my house. Before he arrived that day, he had interacted with somebody (probably a female) who gave him a bad case of the Blue Funk. As a result, he arrived at my home acting "sideways and upside-down" if you know what I mean. I got in his face and said, "You ain't bringing that bullshit in my house, do you hear me?" He understood. Then we were able to take care of business with the music I had planned for that afternoon.

Speaking of females, there was one in particular who was a latter-day version of *The Emperor's New Clothes*. In her case, she was The Empress who somehow got inside Danny's cranium and convinced him that she was the greatest thing since Thomas Edison invented the light bulb which means, of course, that she was Danny's light bulb to turn on and off. Instead of using her real name I'll call her Pretendessa the Invisible.

I will spare you the juicy details of that Tasmanian devil-like dervish. He didn't have a clue about Pretendessa's real objective after entering his life. He also had a personal cheering team rooting for her—not him. She was so amused at having everyone fooled, but she wasn't fooling me and she knew it. Trying to hip Danny to what was happening was like attempting to convince a bird that it is really a boa constrictor by nature. The day finally came when Pretendessa cut the umbilical cord that she bought at the hardware store. At first he was in the Twilight Zone long after Rod Serling had moved elsewhere. It's precisely why I tell Danny, to this day, that his life can be described in two parts— pre-Pretendessa and post-Pretendessa. For several years, he lost that personal audacity he had when we first met and I wondered if he'd get it back.

The good news is that I can tell he's en route to the pre-1980 Danny Lewis audacity. He also knows that he can count on me to be there as his friend by being complimentary or critical when he needs it. So many times he has said to me, "Leonard, that's why I dig you because you always give it to me straight." It's an unconditional friendship that I value, too.

Leonard King, Jr., a.k.a. Dr. Prof. Leonard King

I've had a lot of relationships with women. I jump into their worlds to get to know them, but they don't do likewise when faced with mine. They tend not to travel outside themselves and split when they come face to face with my lifelong mistress. I've had to water down and abbreviate conversations with some girlfriends, and I don't mean that in an elitist or sexist way. What I'm saying is that I haven't always chosen wisely. I've invited self-absorbed and disinterested visitors into my world...like the neighborhood kids who really didn't want to hear the music I played. Even though I've met most romantic interests in music venues, few of them have been more than superficially plugged in, or even cared to be, where my music is concerned. No deep dive is necessary. I could make do with a girlfriend's sincere interest. Few relationships have provided an intimate connection. There was only one woman I could relate to on a level of deep understanding. She had an appreciation of meditation and Eastern philosophy. She dug Coltrane, Davis and Wayne Shorter. Then, as life would have it, she moved to New York City because of her job.

So much time has been spent on what I thought were engaging conversations only to discover later that nothing had registered on the other end. There have been times when I was so in need of intimacy, so in love with being in love and driven by hormones, that I covered my eyes and plugged my ears as I marched head-long into predictably doomed relationships. Psychological blinders have led me into some disappointing, even heartbreak-ing, relationships.

> **When you naturally have a healing aura, you attract a lot of damaged people, and having them in your life could drain your energy to the max... a reminder that it's not your job to heal everyone. You can't pour from an empty cup.**
> *Christopher Walken*

Most of the women whose lives have intersected with mine romantically became involved with me for other reasons. My physical state attracts women who want to help me. I'm told that I emit a tender vibe, and it seems to attract women who are damaged. The damaged ones are needy themselves. Some have seen me as an opportunity for misery-loves-company. Others see me as a shaman who is capable of healing their wounded souls. These relationships sap my energy and pull me down. It's not my job to heal them nor is it theirs to heal that which is not to be healed.

My own relationship shortcomings include staying too long at the fair because of my own ego, continuing a relationship because I think I can lead a damaged soul to the light. I've willingly tripped into fallen sparrow syndrome. Dan, savior and hero, so full of shit. The question is whether I've done this for them or for myself.

Student Repellent

"Damn it, Dan! I'm losing money because of you!" Larry Fratangelo blames me for lost income in 1977, and I guess he should. We live in the same neighborhood on Grosse Ile. Larry's percussion students come to his home where I'm frequently present, "like a lamp," he says. Some of his students are good-looking girls. Not being one to miss an opportunity for a date, I've become involved with a few of them. It's usually nothing serious and therefore short-lived, but I really dig a couple of them. We discuss rhythms and Latin music. One of them plays classical piano, and we go to concerts together. There's common interest and an intellectual connection. They're percussion students after all, as opposed to girlfriends who aren't into music and couldn't care less. When these relationships fizzle out, the girls dump their instructor to avoid running into me. It's not that we split on a sour note or with hard feelings. It's just a matter of avoiding awkward encounters.

Larry and I have been besties since 1976. He's a pain in my ass, and as you can tell, I'm also a pain in his.

Fantasy Loves

A delusional man, I'm forever in love with a long deceased woman who had the most angelic voice I've ever heard...lilting, mystical and timeless. She was taken from us much too soon. This seems to happen with unearthly artists, as if they're briefly shared with us, shooting stars that burn out quickly. Sandy Denny (1947-1978) might be the closest I'll ever come to a love supreme. In case you know Sandy's personal history and are thinking she's a pear in my bucket of love apples, I can tell you it doesn't matter. It's all connected. What could be more pure than this kind of love?

Another woman who occupies my fantasy world of unrequited love is the Girl from Ipanema, Astrud Gilberto. I've daydreamed about the two of us on a beach, total bliss, since the song was released in 1963. I've been into Brazilian music since I was eight and admire the composer Antonio Carlos Jobim, so I attend a performance of his compositions at the Phoenix Center in Pontiac on my birthday. During the concert, Astrud walks into the audience, sits on my lap and sings to me, undoubtedly at the request of my buddies Duduka Da Fonseca, who is performing with her this evening, and Mark Moultrup. I've never sat up so straight in my life. I'm almost levitating. There's just Astrud and me on a white sand beach with ocean waves gently kissing the shore, free from the world below.

Chill and Be Still

We're having a night out in 1984 to catch a performance by Bobby Lewis and the Cracker Jack Band at *Your Mustache Lounge. Mark Conti, my friend since we were kids, is looking a little miffed. He has spent the evening on the prowl without any luck. Like me, Mark has cerebral palsy but less severe. He isn't confined to a wheelchair and walks with crutches. He works out at the gym and he drives. He's independent, has a good job at Detroit Edison, a slick-looking car, great clothes and his own apartment. Unlike me, he did well academ-ically and graduated from an electronics program, having multiple skill sets. He's making his own way without help from anyone.

As always, Mark is revved up to attract girls, his Italian good looks accentuated by dapper fashion. He's handsome and out-going. I, on the other hand, am sitting here quietly wearing a new Saks Fifth Avenue blazer with a spiffy shirt and shoes, enjoying the music and drinks with two pretty girls who are sitting with me to chat. Mark isn't getting any traction and wondering why. No mystery. He's overplaying it. When we get into his Trans Am to go home, he asks, "What do you have that I don't? You just sit there, and girls come to you. I'm out on the dance floor mingling, and no luck." I tell him, "You try too hard. There's no need for clever dialogue or give-and-take glances. I know you just want to score, but let the space around you to breathe. Let them come to you."

Standing in the Shadows of Love (song by the Four Tops)

*Dan Lewis & Friends includes 18 great musicians, so it's no wonder that we catch her attention. We're performing at the 1993 Dally in the Alley, a downtown festival, and sounding good doing Todd Rundgren tunes, fusing rock and jazz. Her eyes meet mine several times during the show, and electricity strikes. She approaches me after the set. "You guys sound great! I really enjoyed the performance." It feels good to attract the interest of a more mature woman, not an impressionable girl from the audience. I ask her, "Would you like to join the band for dinner?" She does, and so it begins...

We're performing frequently at Sully's in Dearborn, and she shows up with some girlfriends. At the end of the evening, she invites me to eat with her and her friends, and I accept a ride with her. On the way to M & M Café, she looks at me and says, "Fuck those assholes. Do you want to go to a hotel?" She proceeds to rock my world. The attraction becomes visceral. As it turns out, I've become involved in an affair with a woman several years older than I, but I don't care. As it also turns out, she's been married for almost forty years, but I don't care about that, either. She's sincerely interested in me, and I gleefully waltz into a seductive vortex. It doesn't take long to learn that she's a highly paid professional who's bored in her marriage. I'm certain she has other boyfriends, but after a while we're exclusive.

Life is wonderful for the first couple of years. She has a great sense of humor, so our time together is always enjoyable. We go on vacations to Traverse City and Atlantic City. She visits me for intimate interludes during lunch breaks. Because of the circumstances and on-the-fly nature of our relationship, I exist on the sidelines of her life...until gradually I awaken to the sobering reality. I'll never be allowed into her mainstream sphere. Allure fades when you become emotionally bankrupt. What have I been thinking? That she would leave her husband of many years? He's a successful businessman, she earns a six-figure income, and together they've amassed a considerable estate, not something she would want to split with him no matter how bored or unhappy she is. Extramarital flings are her coping strategy. It lasts six years because we share an intellectual plane, and the unbridled sexual connection is addictive. Like jazz improv, I've traveled out there and now I must find my way back home. This journey home is very painful.

I learned a lot, so much in fact that I wouldn't do it again. I was happy for a while, but I parked much too long on a dead end street. Whether I wanted to hear it or not, Leonard King counseled me. He was practicing for downtown concerts with about 25 *cats, me among them. We practiced in his basement. If my relationship with a woman wasn't going well, I wore a forlorn expression and my concentration was poor. I repeated this pattern until Leonard went off on me before practice. He described this interaction in the narrative at the beginning of this chapter in gentler terms, but what he actually told me was, "Look, man, don't bring that shit down here. It fucks up the vibe. Why do you allow these distractions? Why do you let them define you? Don't you like yourself? They'll steal your soul. If you're bankrupt, there's nothing you can offer here. The next time you come down here, don't bring us down. Fuck you and your lovesick ass. We've got music to work on." To this day, Leonard is probably disappointed in the way I handle relationships with women. I guess I still have some work to do. I've been hardened by heartbreak, but these days I'm listening and better off for it.

Just Passing Through

It's a bustling day at Borders Books in 2006. I'm sifting through vinyl and CDs in the jazz section, hoping to find some hard bop, specifically Michael Brecker's latest release, when I see her. Immediate allure—beautiful ebony skin and piercing green eyes. As if drawn in my direction by some invisible force, she ventures nearby where she picks up a Kenny G album and turns it over to read track titles. "Awwww...you don't want to do that." The words slip across my tongue before I can block their exit. Pretentious. What a pushy ass I must sound like. Rather than show any irritation, she smiles, and her face lights up with merriment at my bold intrusion. As I'm thinking what a lucky shot I've taken, she responds in a French accent, "*Wheech you soojest?*"

We have an immediate connection. She's a pharmacist from Paris who is in the U.S. visiting friends for two months. Her name is Patience. Believing music is the universal language, I introduce her to the sounds of Miles Davis and Thelonius Monk, and she teaches me that there's a way to relate beyond the spoken word and even beyond music. We get together a couple of times a week for dinner or just coffee. Truth is, we don't need to speak in order to relate on a higher level. All we need is to look into each other's eyes and we both understand perfectly.

Time stands still for two wonderful months that I wish will never end. Patience tells me about France and shares her observation that Americans seldom relax and take in the surroundings...always in a hurry. She lives a laid-back but tuned-in rhythm, so our time together is a breath of fresh air that allows me to cut through daily noise and tune in to tender vibes. We savor each moment, no expectations, no schedule. She welcomes me into an existence where the tempo of life ebbs and flows naturally, never allegro. I learn about her life, and she listens to mine. I'm immersed in a refined European cultural experience, and Patience expands her appreciation of great music. Like everything in life, the rapture ends when the day arrives that we knew would come. Phone calls to Paris become expensive. After a while, our long distance relationship fades.

An Altar Named Reality

They're all sweaty, hovering over me. I can smell their breath and Bay Rum Aftershave. I feel the heat from their bodies as they place their hands on my head, my shoulders, my feet and legs. Their words are unintelligible, voices surging and ebbing, some speaking in such a fevered pitch that saliva spews into the air in small sprays, eyes closed and hands pressing hard against me during their louder entreaties to a higher power.

I'm wondering if she'll be satisfied with my willingness to endure this. To date, she has shown no glimmer of understanding my life and what's important to me. I'm suffering through this exercise in futility for her, knowing what the outcome will be. In spite of the best intentions of the faith healers, my legs remain useless, dangling appendages attached to my stationary ass. I don't leap out of the wheelchair and sprint down the aisle of the church proclaiming, "Thank you, Jesus!" Once outside the church, she asks, "What did you feel?" I simply tell her, "Their body heat." Then she asks, "Do you feel any different?" Having expended all my energy and patience on being subjected to this humiliating experience at her insistence, I slide into realist mode and ask her, "How about accepting me as I am?" Here I go again, announcing that there's no Santa Claus, blowing up her Pentecostal fantasy. She cries, and I make an effort not to roll my eyes.

Did she actually expect a miraculous transformation? From this point on, she distances herself emotionally, remains in denial, and continues to place responsibility on me to change the unchangeable, apparently feeling no need to accept the permanence of my condition. To shed further light on this girl-friend's beliefs, she considers transcendental meditation to be demonic but thinks the laying on of hands and speaking in tongues can heal cerebral palsy.

For 2 1/2 years prior to the faith healing attempt in 2018, it was very difficult for this girlfriend and me to get together because of my living situation. New lodging now allows us to spend more time together, but our relationship is unraveling. She's 15 years younger than I, but our incompatibility is based on more than the age difference. I've begun to accept what I've purposely been ignoring. She's damaged and intellectually handicapped. Her mindset about my physical condition smacks of the Evangelical belief that gay and lesbian persons should be rehabilitated. The faith healing scene reminds me of the guru Ali Baba many years ago in New York City when he said bathing me in oil would heal me and I would walk the streets of the city (Chapter 6: Escapades & Escapes, section Smoke and Snake Oil). The difference is that Ali Baba was a flimflam man who actually knew better.

What was I thinking when I got into this relationship? I still wonder, mostly out of ego, whether I eventually could have cracked her mindset so she could understand that God doesn't intend for me to walk and that I must live with the strengths and abilities that I actually have. I do have faith and believe in prayer, but there will be no miracle here. In addition to all this, I'm a music snob. This woman and her friends enjoy karaoke, and that alone should have been the first clue to our hopeless mismatch.

Wary Heart

I admire the longevity of Edgar Winter's relationship with his wife, Monique. They've been together for over 35 years. We talked about it once, and he told me he was fortunate to find someone who understands him and will hang in there with him. I envy that!

Can deep understanding co-exist with romantic love? I'd like to believe it's possible, but it ain't lookin' good for me so far. Time hasn't been kind, and my relationships with women don't seem to be moving in an upward direction. Leonard considers those relationships to be symptoms of me feeling beaten down. He sees most of them as destructive forces that have interfered with my spirit and my potential. I play into the mike, but the speakers are off. Sometimes it's me who turned them off. Tower of Power wrote lyrics about being unable to walk a straight line if you're wearing crooked shoes ("Get Yo Feet Back on the Ground"). I guess that's me, and I can't blame anyone but myself. Paul Simon described what goes on in my head when he wrote "50 Ways to Leave Your Lover."

The pair, the two who are one
Our journey to nowhere
Will end when we get there

From the poem "Universal" in Memoirs de Nocturne:
An Anthology by Abe Sulfaro
(1970-2014), Detroit musician, author and poet

I used to wear blinders but no longer. Here's my self-psycho-analysis: Relationships with women have been substitutes for a normal life and what I've desired in a career. I no longer expect to meet the "right person" ... if I ever did. Suzanne Lewis knew this and lovingly told me.

CHAPTER THIRTEEN
Melody & Harmony

**If you play music with passion and love and honesty, then
it will nourish your soul, heal your wounds, and make
your life worth living. Music is its own reward.**

Sting

Pat Metheny told me, "There are a lot of guys out there who
are just as good as I am. They're out there playing every
night." There are world class *cats in Detroit who could,
and some do, perform on national and international stages.
They've dedicated their lives to being the best, living their craft.
They're masters. For them, it's like breathing. Some of the musicians in this chapter are Detroiters and some are not. Each one
is closely connected in my heart. Among the greats they are...

Al Ayoub—Guitarist

*Dan Lewis & Friends began in 1990. It took a long time to put
a big band together. I auditioned several guitarists including Dan
Mayer and Chuck Silva, Norma Bell's guitarist who was playing at
*Axels at 8-Mile and Evergreen and selling shoes to supplement
his income. Because he was so busy, Chuck referred me to Al

Ayoub. Al was excited to have been called, trying to make a living while caring for his father. Here's a *cat who in just two days actually listened to all the tunes I'd sent him. The first time I heard Al play, he blew me away. Fortunately, he saw potential in my vision. Our first few gigs drew him in, not to mention that we had nice rehearsal spaces and everyone was paid on time in personal envelopes. With Al in our midst, *Dan Lewis & Friends delivered memorable performances. He has always worked alongside me, making my vision his own. Through his connections, we played at the Focus: HOPE benefit for two years.

As Al and I got to know each other, he became more interested in me. He's one curious son of a bitch. We talked about life, philosophy and religion. He wanted to know what made me tick, and now that he does, he peels me like an onion.

There's nothing Al can't do, not only on stage but also at home and in other settings. At the 2015 Detroit Jazz Festival, Al was playing with jazz guitarist Pat Metheny, the festival's artist in residence. During rehearsal, Pat needed help setting up the computer system to run a video memorializing German double bassist Eberhard Weber. It included a complex piece of music for the grand finale. With the exception of conductor-pianist Alan Broadbent, everyone in the orchestra appeared clueless to the fact that Pat was in need of assistance, and valuable rehearsal time was being lost. Al asked Pat, "Would you like some help?" and got down on the floor with him to get the program synchronized with a live orchestra. Pat said he couldn't have done it without out Al, and I really doubt the rehearsal would have taken place without his technical know-how. If at all possible, Al will find a way to fix things and make them better. He has worked with companies abroad to expand guitar synthesizer technologies.

As a guitarist, Al has performed with Neil Sedaka, Kool & the Gang, Little Anthony and the Imperials and many others. He ingeniously adapts electric and acoustic guitars to symphonic arrangements for the Detroit Symphony Orchestra and symphonies across the country. In doing so, he has created a genre. Al has supersonic ears that hear everything. During a performance, there's no over-playing, and yet he brings something to the music every time, a true *cat in every sense of the word. When he solos, melody is first. He adapts to the band, and it's always right. Al doesn't behave like he's the only one on stage. He plays with the group and is willing to let the others shine, sharing the stage naturally just as he lives.

Dan on congas, Al Ayoub right on guitar.
Jazz festival, Grosse Ile, MI, 1990

Al and I truly have become brothers. We've always argued and still do. I can't tell you how many times we've hung up on each other. I tell him to go fuck himself, and he calls me Ass Hat. Then we kiss and make up, often with a deeper mutual understanding. Al gives back, no one-way street with him. He gets involved in your personal life because that's the only way he knows how to roll as a friend and brother. When things were really bad with my mother and I had to be relocated, he moved me into his home and helped me get into a temporary assisted living facility. When times are tough, he soldiers on and gets it done, focused and selfless. Al doesn't walk away. He's a humanitarian who feels a calling to help others.

For almost thirty years, Al has been a steadfast confidant. I was the best man at his wedding. In spite of our brotherly arguments, he's closer than a blood sibling, someone who can finish my sentences, and I love him. He always looks out for me like a doctor who knows how to take care of things. Forever grateful.

Roy Brooks (1938-2005)—Percussionist

"There's no wrong rhythm, Dan. You're transmitting energy, positive or negative." Memorable words of strength and support from a dear mentor.

We met in 1982 through Leonard King. It seemed to intrigue Roy that like Leonard, who started playing drums at the age of twelve, I began at the age of eight. Roy taught me to treat drums as if they're a piano. The more tones you can make with your hands the better, sound transmission depending on how you attack percussive instruments. He advised me to work on muscle tone. He took the time to listen and give me feedback on my performances, and he taught me about tonality and variations of *Guaguancó. He counseled me to trust my own voice in percussion. "You gave your soul to this long before now. We're all warriors." Through this great musician, I was inspired to imagine and to become a messenger. He told me, "You can compose and play concertos on drums."

Roy was a cultural anthropologist who used drums like ancient messengers used them to communicate between African villages. He wrote "The Mystical Afro Knot," a piece that he personified, living proof of the ability to speak through drums, telling a story. He masterfully delivered classical African rhythms, reverberating indigenous roots. Roy had another gift, too. Upon entering a room, he could read the crowd. His reading drove his delivery. His performances stood alone, bringing drums to the forefront as a lead instrument.

Roy and I shared the same birthday, both of us Pisces. Sometimes he'd call on our birthday and I'd hear, "Coming to you from underwater," as he made a gurgling sound. I miss you, brother.

Ending Note at the end of this book is a brief anecdote capturing the essence of the unique human being and artist, Roy Brooks.

Larry Fratangello—Percussionist

"You're born alone and you die alone." If it's possible to make that statement affectionately to a friend, it's spoken in that vein by Larry. You've probably noticed that many of the experiences, adventures and mishaps in this book have been with Larry Fratangelo. He told me many years ago, "Look, asshole. I'll be your legs." He has the grit to stand up to any challenge and has taught me to do the same—even though some of our escapades might lead one to question our judgment. I've had more disagreements with Larry than anyone. He hits me square between the eyeballs. "Nobody gives a shit if you have cerebral palsy." This may or may not be true, but Larry for sure doesn't. He's not one to soft pedal harsh realities either. "Dan, people are going to do whatever the fuck they're going to do, and it has nothing to do with you. They'll mess with your groove. Don't let 'em."

I met Larry 44 years ago (1976) through Ali Mora (later known as Francisco Mora) when they were playing at a Detroit club called Perfect Blend and also at *Cobb's Corner on Cass Avenue. I was playing okay at the time but was feeling hemmed in and stuck by physical limitations. I needed to tighten up on rhythms in general and had insurmountable barriers related to my legs. I also wanted to become more familiar with Latin rhythms and add more percussion instruments to my repertoire. Ali referred me to the percussionist with the group Cordova for instruction, a guy named Larry Fratangelo who coincidentally lived near me.

Larry is one of the finest percussionists I've ever known, and he's also one of the best teachers I've ever had. He meets you where you live and pushes you to your uppermost limit. Larry opened gateways for me not only in music but also in life where improvisation is an everyday coping and survival skill. Rhythmic improv is a transportation vehicle, destination freedom, and with Larry's help it led me to a contemplative plane. He'd play rhythms over verbal stories, literally interpreting them with drums, and I'd answer in rhythm. In this way, we've shared virtual exploration—canoeing, hiking, walking in the forest and time travel. I've imagined what it would feel like to stand for the first time, even feeling that physical experience. I've been on my feet, walking, observing the surroundings with total absence of weight. It's the greatest distance I've ever traveled outside myself, and with it has come freedom inside myself through limitless imaginings. This is where improvisation takes you, and Larry led the way for me. From him, I've learned how to get inside a vision, a hidden world that comes to life and a dimension that you don't see at first.

Larry plays percussion like a piano, melodiously, making it a lead instrument. His percussion is at times lightning in a bottle and at other times a tapestry, taking every measure and finding the place where it fits, everything merging with precision. Larry understands classical structure but doesn't employ it because for him it's more important to develop and master his own style. He's been recorded on more albums and hit records than most drummers because artists and producers recognize that he makes a tune come to life by adding special ingredients, like baking a gourmet *soufflé* without overdoing any ingredient. He has influenced drummers the likes of Chad Smith of the Red Hot Chili Peppers, Dennis Chambers, Jonathan Mover, Tyrone Lampkin of Funkadelic and others. You immediately know it's Larry when you hear a recording. His percussion breathes entirely on its own like a newborn baby, drawing the listener in.

Larry Fratangelo

Larry is prescient. His prediction during the disco era: Melodic instruments will take a back seat, and drums will be front and center. The drum will interpret everything. We'll become slaves to rhythm and time. Pop rhythms will come out of computers.

He's an exploratory musician, especially as it relates to Afro-Cuban rhythms. He conceived Drum Devils in 1990 with George Bennett and Dennis Sheridan. Their percussive orchestra eventually grew from 3 to 25 to 50. I'm so proud of how this group, a rhythmic troupe for street performances, was created and developed. Its sounds are raw yet beautiful, even using crude instruments such as tin cans and garbage cans. It starts in the street and stays there, authentic urban percussion with a collage of rhythms, cascading complex time signatures. Within this pursuit, Larry has taught me about *Cascara, *Bembé, *Guaguancó, *Merengue and *Clave. Beyond that, he has led me to a better understanding of his passion, indigenous Afro-Cuban rhythm, which he composes and performs fluently. In classic Fratangelo fashion, Drum Devils stretches boundaries and opens magical landscapes.

Larry has taken care of me, watched out for me and included me more times than I can write about here. His friendship has bridged music pursuits with personal needs during dark periods in my life. He's tough on me, cuts me no slack. Like a brother, he's a pain in my ass, and I'm a pain in his. Larry tells me, "We've got to work together even though our lives aren't always enjoyable and we face struggles. We're not done yet." In the earthy ways that belong only to him, Larry gives me comfort and hope. His indelible touch is forever etched into cherished experiences, my psyche and my heart.

Leonard King, Jr.—Drummer, band leader, mentor

Leonard is a Detroit music great and music historian. I'd seen and heard him perform before we actually met. He played with the Lyman Woodard Organization, and I followed Lyman (1942-2009) around. I used to go to hear the group at the *Fort Shelby Hotel. One night in that intimate setting, rare and unforgettable moments took place when Charles Mingus and his band members sat in with Lyman's group.

Leonard and I met in 1976 when he was a radio personality at WDET public radio on the campus of Wayne State University. I used to listen to Full Circle, his music broadcast. In those days, public radio gave local musicians airplay, so of course Leonard was someone I wanted to meet. He was a dynamic and engaging radio personality, very inviting. I found out that he was, and is, the same man in person. Horizon, my band at the time, had recorded a performance at the Trenton Theater, and I knew Leonard would be interested. My instincts were right. I called him, and he told me to come down to the station. I played a recording of Horizon doing "Treat" by Santana for him. Leonard and I hit it off, and thereafter we performed and recorded together on several of his projects, some of them finding international airplay.

Leonard has put together multiple groups over the decades including the Strata Nova Orchestra which I was invited to join in the '80s. His basement was a music laboratory where I witnessed how improvisation can deliver anything that's desired. Through Leonard, I got to know so many Detroit musicians. When several notables were just getting started, Leonard mentored them and drew out the best in them—Regina Carter, James Carter and Rodney Whitaker, all now internationally known performers. Strata Nova Orchestra performed live during several broadcasts of Full Circle. The atmosphere was electric during those shows that combined Leonard's commentary, Q & A and live music at the WDET studio. There's nothing like a live broadcast to get your adrenaline pumpin'. When that red light clicks on—On the Air—it's immediate, powerful and in real time, a dose of high energy, demanding that you bring your best because there's no safety net. Spontaneity produces positive anxiety that keeps you on your toes. Leonard also used his broadcast to plug artists and gigs, familiarizing listeners with the musicians.

Dan and Leonard at Cliff Bell's Jazz Club, Detroit, 2020
Photo by Jamie Heilman

Starting his own independent record label, Uuquipleu (pronounced yoo-kee-ploo) Records, has been an entrepreneurial triumph for Leonard. I applaud him for taking control of his own destiny. He has also preserved Lyman Woodard's legacy through the Lyman Woodard Organization for the Arts, keeping Lyman's artistry as an organist and composer alive and expanding his international reach. People all over the world enjoy Lyman's music because of what Leonard has done.

Leonard is steadfast and loyal. He kept me on even after missteps on my part, including distractions related to women and other embarrassing incidents. When his band was playing on the moonlight cruise to Boblo Island, I wheeled myself into a corner for privacy to use the urinal that I carry. Thinking I was emptying it over the side of the double-decker ferry into the Detroit River, I instead dumped the urine onto a dance floor below. Seeing what I was about to do, Leonard's guys yelled, "Dan, no!" but it was too late as I heard a man's voice below yell, "What's leaking?"

My friendship with Leonard continues to this day because I listened to my inner voice and called him in 1976—and because he's a warm, welcoming human being. Leonard didn't care about my handicap when we met, and he still doesn't. With Leonard, you either hang as a fellow *cat or you don't. No mollycoddling. Take your fuckin' lumps. Probably the greatest testament to Leonard King, in addition to being a stellar musician and music historian, is the success of the people he has pushed to excel. He focuses on character and musicianship, no free passes. He's a great teacher and mentor who has guided me to earn the respect of musicians and to become a full status *cat. I'll always be grateful to Leonard for giving me the opportunity to work with him. Because of him, I've become a better musician and I hope a better man.

Bobby Lewis (Norman Warner)—Guitarist, composer, Detroit music legend

We met in 1975 at a bar called *Your Mustache on Michigan Avenue in Dearborn when he was performing with Bobby Lewis and the Cracker Jack Band. As this book is being written, Bobby is visiting at my house where I'm stuck in bed with a fractured tibia. He arrived at 2:00 pm and stayed with me until 10:00 pm. He has been a constant in my life. When we're together in person, there's so much to talk about and so many things to catch up on that we usually have to continue in a phone call later. Solid and invaluable, he always understands what I'm trying to accomplish, but our friendship goes beyond music. We have conversations about anything that's on our minds. He enriches my life with his caring, giving nature. He acknowledges my musicianship and the music history that's stored in my head. He says I should write a column called "Dan Says."

Bobby is a virtuoso with dedication to craft. He was a member of The Headliners when they signed with Motown Records in 1964 and later formed Bobby Lewis and the Cracker Jack Band. He was in *Dan Lewis & Friends for a while and recorded with me. He's amazing, still performing at 80 years of age.

Bobby has long been and continues to be one of my most cherished influences. He has given me much good advice about making a living as a musician, and he should know, having put kids through college. His guidance has been an asset through heart-breaks in the music business and has even included the skills and values needed for just being a man. He gently beats me up when I make shaky decisions. These qualities have made Bobby Lewis a respected, charismatic leader. His wife is writer and photographer

Bobby Lewis with The Headliners, 1964, on the steps of Hitsville U.S.A., originally the home of Berry Gordy and Motown Records on West Grand Boulevard, Detroit, MI, now the Motown Museum. (L to R): Bobby Lewis (guitar and vocals), Ray Clayton (saxophone, flute, keyboard), Larrie Londin (drums), Lonnie Londin (bass, front man)

Jan Warner. His daughter, Gia Warner, is a well known Detroit singer-songwriter and music producer. His daughter Wendy is a music teacher in North Carolina. The Warner family has been an integral, consistent part of my life for the past 45 years.

Dave Liebman—Saxophonist, flutist, composer, arranger, educator

A jazz *cat in the purest sense. I have the greatest respect and gratitude for Dave. I admired him before I knew him, as far back as Ten Wheel Drive, and have enjoyed his many records over the years. I could always feel the power in Dave's music, but knowing him as a man, a friend, is one of the pleasures in my life. Dave and his wife, Caris Visentin Liebman (oboist, composer, educator), have never let me down and have graciously included me in events. When Elvin Jones died, I couldn't be present at the funeral service, so Dave allowed me to listen in on his phone.

I've learned from Dave that there's structure to responsible improvisation. In order to travel outside, you must first go inside. The journey swirls around a melody and chords with a varied palette of notes. You can go out there, but you have to know how to get back to the original theme. As a musician, composer and educator, Dave pursues excellence and will settle for nothing less. He exudes the prana of John Coltrane and Miles Davis. Dave was in Miles' band during the transition, fusing rock and jazz—revolutionary—breaking new ground and changing the landscape of jazz. Dave told me he also grew as a musician when working with Elvin Jones, Coltrane's drummer. "When you're able to work closely with masters, there's nothing better. It kept my improvisation quest open, no limits."

Dave always gives me the truth in classic New York fashion, no bullshit or mincing words. He speaks of music as the miracle it is without skipping over its realities, helping me recognize several layers in any situation. He has kept me in the loop with his pursuits and given me truth related to mine. His unpolished wisdom sometimes catches me off guard, but it always keeps me on track. I take advice from few people, and Dave Liebman is one of them. He has given me legs for life and has taught me to trust myself, to listen to my inner voice and not to compromise.

Scott Morgan—Rock 'n roll, soul and R&B musician

In the 1960s, if you could get a record played on Detroit radio, it might break (find broader airplay) regionally, especially in the Cleveland market, and even internationally. Rosalie Trombley, program director at CKLW, was often instrumental in making that happen. An Ann Arbor, Michigan band known as The Rationals (Scott Morgan, Steve Correll, Terry Trabandt, Bill Figg) used that pathway and would occasionally appear on "Swinging Time," a TV dance show out of Windsor, Ontario on the Canadian side of the Detroit River. It was hosted by Robin Seymour, a CKLW radio personality who was The Rationals' manager for a while. They were White guys playing R&B akin to Black artists such as Eddie Holland and Chuck Jackson. When The Rationals performed R&B classics, they'd rock 'em up while maintaining their authenticity. They made a regional hit of Otis Redding's "Respect." I continued to follow Scott when he was with Sonic Rendezvous (Fred "Sonic" Smith of the MC5, Gary Rasmussen, Scott Asheton). I idolized Scott Morgan then and still do. He can sing a ballad or R&B tune with the voice and vibe of Black singers.

Thirty years after first hearing Scott, I decided to call him. Even though *Dan Lewis & Friends didn't play anything similar to his repertoire, I asked him to do a couple of songs with us at the *Magic Bag. He agreed and found himself on stage with jazz *cats—a musical mismatch. Scott did a Rationals song, "Guitar Army." I don't know whether he thought it worked or not, but I love him and was honored to be on stage with him! To this day, I'm grateful for his willingness to perform with us. He's gracious, a prince. He never questioned what he was walking into, so he didn't know it was an 18-piece big band. He jumped in like a warrior because he knew what it meant to me, and that, Scott, is why you've endeared yourself to me.

Mark Murphy (1932-2015)—Jazz singer and lyricist

I first heard Mark at *Baker's Keyboard Lounge around 1975-76. Having some of his records, I loved his purist, authentic approach. He'd been singing since the '50s when he was on Capitol Records doing the genre flavor of the day—vanilla. He made a few pop records, but they didn't do that well. He preferred Black music, specifically bebop jazz. Because he wouldn't stay in the lane where they'd placed him, Capitol dropped him. In the '60s, he forged his own path in bebop and improvisational *scat singing. If you're an authentic jazz singer in the spirit of Maxine Sullivan and King Pleasure, to name a couple of Mark's idols, you embrace it for its own sake.

Mark made tough choices about profit versus doing what you feel, choices that made him an artist whose talent far exceeded his fame. He kept the music untarnished and rejected commercialism. He recorded approximately fifty albums, two of them tributes to Nat King Cole. Mark was bold about being a purist.

Nothing was watered down. He became a jazz insider's insider, a world nomad and road warrior who for fifty years made a living playing small clubs and concerts.

Getting to know Mark was an enlightening journey, particularly related to genre, the true meaning of improvisation and taking chances. With him as a teacher who lived what he espoused, I observed in real time, over a period of about ten years, the hard realities of jazz and the music business. Mark allowed me inside his life as a performer, accompanying him on some smaller scale however memorable road trips. It was through Mark that I got to know Shirley Horn and stay at her home in Washington, D.C. Mark stayed at my house when he played at *Baker's Lounge in Detroit. When I think of him, I gratefully recall a man who provided passage for me to become closer to the music. To this day, I respect him for sticking with his passion, forging a craft out of improv and creating a style distinctly his own.

Andy Newmark—Percussionist

"Dan, are you ready to go sailing on the SS Dandrew?" Andy has helped me weather some rough storms, hence his reference to a fantasy seagoing vessel. It's an inside joke hatched by Andrew. We still talk about what will become of that imaginary yacht when we both die. One of the aspects of Andy's personality that I enjoy most is his perverse sense of humor because it matches mine. We're cynics at heart.

I met Andy through Bobby Lewis in 1978. Our first in-person interaction was in New York City where we met at a deli for lunch. After that, we would connect during my visits to the city. I could feel that I mattered to Andy then and still do. At one point, we talked almost daily. Our conversations have covered subjects related to self-discovery, growth, life and human potential. We can and do talk about anything. I'm always glad we've consulted each other and not necessarily about life circumstances. We also talk about music projects, reviewing the pros and cons. Through these dialogues, a bond and trust have grown between us. Andy serves as a sounding board, bringing clarity to any project's potential in facts and figures before I wade in deeper. He encourages me to look at situations from different angles. This works in a bi-directional manner, and I've given him advice, too. We don't always agree, but he's an honest, trustworthy friend I can always turn to. I think he feels the same way about me.

Andy is one of the most widely utilized session drummers in the world. Because he's so talented, it's hard for me to accept that, like others who've spent many years performing, he has chosen to kick back somewhat. I'm so comfortable with him that I forget he's an accomplished drummer with international reach. I'm a lousy fan, and to Andy's credit, that's not what he's about or what our friendship is based on. He lives in London, England these days, but we still talk occasionally. He remains a trusted confidant and will always hold a special place in my heart.

Dan Oestrike—Bass guitarist, arranger, producer

We met in 1975 when Dan was in the band Scott with Derek St. Holmes on guitar and Brian Statfield on drums. I used to go hear Scott when they were shaking up the town, opening for well known rock groups in the early '70s at places like the *Michigan Palace, the Painted Pony (Brownstown Township), *Lincoln Park Theater and Carraway Ballroom. Scott was like Cream, three musicians who played off each other, each one knowing where the other was going and allowing the music to be their vehicle. Like jazz *cats, they never played a tune the same way twice. Dan was exciting on stage. He'd bravely take a bass solo and improvise with trust in his fellow band members, and Derek and Brian trusted him to do the same for them. He elevated rhythm to another level and put a new spin on electric bass, stretching it out without sounding repetitive. I desperately wanted to meet Dan and to become friends. He was everything I wanted to be as a musician, one who can speak through his instrument. He truly got it about improv, always fresh and interesting with unbridled energy on stage, unapologetic about his aggressive solos. He went out there as a vessel that serves the music. I knew then he would be transformative in my life, a mentor.

Dan and I became brothers and have supported each other through many rough patches. He understands my need for continual intellectual growth and engages me in dialogues about philosophy, neuroscience, ambient sound, tonality, sound textures, composers and avant-garde and classical music. We don't always come to the same conclusions, but after lengthy and intense conversations, we might reach agreement or we might go to the library, the place Dan calls "the real source." After a 45-year friendship, we're still having those talks. We have deep discussions that provide a pillar in my life constructed of straight talk and insights. He knows my potential has been severely hampered by dyslexia, and we used to spend hours in the Dearborn library where he'd read to me.

Dan's family has embraced me, and I've always felt a part of them. He's hard working and dedicated, not afraid to tackle anything. He has performed in many bands over the years, and he's constantly moving upward toward perfection no matter how long it takes, a man after my own heart. Dan is active in studio projects and continues to explore the bass, keeping modern ears and never stopping. He doesn't always recognize his impact, but I see him as a warrior.

Michael Royal—Jazz pianist, composer, arranger, jazz scholar

I met Michael when I went to visit my father in Florida. Dad began attending Michael's performances when emphysema prevented him from golfing. He told Michael about me and sent Michael's CDs to me, so I was well versed in his music before we met. Related to this section about Michael, I need to express how grateful I am to my father for finally taking an interest in my music. Only after moving to Florida and meeting Michael Royal did he begin to appreciate my knowledge of the American art form known as jazz. It was a gateway of sorts for us because in his later years, my father and I became better friends and talked on a more introspective level. This was due in large part to Michael Royal.

Michael got into jazz in his early 20s and toured the world. Those experiences, plus his ongoing broad-based study and natural ability to connect with people, prepared and enabled him to lecture on jazz at colleges and other venues. He's a bebopper, a Charlie Parker and Dizzy Gillespie devotee, forever in the trenches and always scholarly. He has included me when he's in the process of researching and preparing lectures. We bounce ideas off each other. He's gracious, open and collaborative however uncompromising on the important things. Thanks to Michael, my music interests expanded to include classical composers such

Dan with Michael Royal at the Ritz Carlton,
Sarasota, Florida, 1993

as Bach, Vivaldi, Beethoven and Mozart, and I realized that I'd
never given classical music its due.

Michael and I had phone calls when I wasn't in Florida, and our
conversations weren't just about music. He introduced me to the
works of writers, poets, philosophers and playwrights including
John Velon, James Hillman, William Blake and Eugene O'Neill,

challenging me to broaden my exposure to varying perspectives and abstract thinking.

Having experience with hospice work, Michael helped me cope with my mother's illness and death. He had learned to allow people who are near the end of life to tell their stories. He told me there would be times when Mom would reach back into her memory with clarity, and she did. Michael had met my mother before she developed Alzheimer's. He considered her a pillar of strength and admired her understanding of my passion for music. When she was becoming sick, she read some of the literature that Michael sent to me including philosopher John Velon (becoming as opposed to being) and psychologist James Hillman (archetypal psychology, fantasies and myths that shape our psychological lives). He also sent books on Native American spiritual concepts, going beyond self, shifting the paradigm and allowing portals to open. Mom would sit in a rocking chair and read those books aloud. It was comforting to me, too. She had the ability to look at a concept from all angles, one of the sharpest people I've ever known even in her decline. Michael admired these traits in Suzanne not to mention that she used to play piano. My sisters and I were having a hard time as our mother to wandered farther and farther into a place where it was difficult to reach her. Michael told me, "Look, Dan. It's just another way of thinking. Your mom's molecules are changing. Accept her for who she's becoming and respect her journey." I learned to let Mom be in her own dimension. Michael helped me with all this. Just before she died, he told me she was still a shining beacon.

Through the great philosophers, Michael helped me refine my cognitive processing. He was a task master when I ventured back into old ways of thinking that cause self-sabotage. Over time, the paradigm shifts, and you conquer your demons. I owe Michael so much for encouraging me to move closer to self-actualization. I've continued to think more deeply about human behavior and how to approach dilemmas. Challenges and unpleasant things in life become manageable when tackling them through a more evolved way of thinking. Michael always encourages me to pursue a meaningful relationship with myself and the world around me. He was a serious Buddhist for many years and lived in Japan for two years, Eastern philosophy being another connection between us. We're communicating in the same manner after 25 years. From him I've learned to empower myself, to avoid the herd mentality, and to consider life from different perspectives.

Gary Schunk (1954-2021)—Pianist, composer, arranger, music historian

Your unexpected passing as this book is being completed hits me hard. You will leave an indelible imprint on the landscape of Detroit jazz forever.

I don't recall where Gary and I met in 1976, but we were simpatico right off. He's one of the finest pianists I've ever heard, in a class with Herbie Hancock, Bill Evans and Denny Zeitlin. Gary is so good, in fact, that others are intimidated. He has played internationally, sharing the stage with Charles McPherson, Sonny Stitt, Branford Marsalis, Mark Murphy, Marcus Belgrave, Jimmy Ponder, Dave Liebman, Peter Erskine and many others.

Gary is soft spoken and understated, and yet he shines brightly. He's one of the greats, a great writer and arranger and a great classical pianist with a signature style that you recognize right away. He told me, "It helps for a jazz pianist to have a classical background. It expands your palette melodically and helps you make harmony a priority. It gives European influence to the Western art form." He transcends by delving into all jazz genres. This *cat also knows how to fuse rock and jazz! In addition, he's a jazz and classical music scholar.

More contemporary than others and constantly testing limits, Gary pushes boundaries and forges new frontiers. He's a modern *cat, intrigued by electronic innovations, continually seeking new gear and striving to keep the music fresh. As a performer, he pulls the audience in and enthralls them. He appeared on Mark Murphy's two Nat King Cole tribute albums and has recorded with multiple other artists. He has formed multiple groups and has released several of his own CDs including *Kayak* (Peter Erskine and The Gary Schunk Trio) and *Key Player*.

Even though there's an aura around him, Gary seems unaware of his personal power. He has introduced me to many musicians around Detroit and has helped me understand the politics in this city, how it can throw up barriers. We delve into life, civics and people. He has helped me, and I've helped him. I was the best man at his wedding. Gary is one of the best friends I've ever had, like a brother, as close now as when we first met.

Ron Smith (1959-2015)—Guitarist

We met in 1977 through George Clinton. Ron was a Funkadelic devotee who knew as much about the group as George did. Ron also lived and breathed Motown, leading me to understand its history. His father was Bobbie Smith, one of the founding members of The Spinners. In the '90s, Ron joined them as a guitarist. Through him, I got to know Motown artists and their inside stories as well as the music's roots and its impact. We shared a broad and deep interest in R&B. He loved playing guitar and idolized

Jimi Hendrix. He would occasionally come to hear *Dan Lewis and Friends.

Ron had been separated from Bobbie for many years and lived with his maternal grandmother. Even after re-establishing a relationship with his father, he felt alone and was experiencing uncertainties in his life. He and I found commonality in our mutual discontent with the state of our lives and the challenges of the music business. We formed a support group of two and lifted each other up. We spoke deep truths, not just about life's challenges and hardships but also about our strengths. In doing so, we became life coaches for each other.

Ron wore blinders when it came to himself. He didn't recognize his own capabilities, relying on others to advance his visions and pursuits. All the years with his grandmother hadn't prepared him for independence. When he toured with The Spinners, he always had a hole in his pocket and no plan for tomorrow, realizing later in his adult life that you can't depend on others to take care of you. After being estranged from his father for so many years, he was grateful and proud to be playing with The Spinners. It was more important to him than anything. Ron did little self-help beyond our little support group of two. He had a lot more going for himself than he realized. He had his own band, Enemy Squad, that played venues across the country and opened for major acts. My advice to him: Get yourself into a position where you're not beholden to others and take control of your own destiny.

Over the years, Ron's dad and The Spinners extended many courtesies to me. At an outdoor performance in Flint, Michigan, the event coordinator tried to seat the mayor and his party in the front row, taking a spot reserved for me. I was being side-lined in favor of the dignitaries. Ron saw what was happening and intervened. When he was told, "These seats are for the mayor's guests," he responded firmly, "No. This spot is Dan's. He's with us." The Spinners never compromised. If I was there, I was one of them, period. At some performances, I was with them on stage, in the wings. Ron always had my back and was my advocate. People can be intrusive and inconsiderate. If someone approached us and started talking to me about my disability, he'd tell them in gritty, street-tough terms, "Look, mother fucker, this guy is a musician and music historian. That's what we're talking about, so unless you have something to add to our conversation, just keep walkin'."

From Ron I learned deep Detroit. We cobbled together coping strategies for life. Ron revealed street level realities to me, and I was his sounding board and a source of strength when he was feeling defeated. He needed confidence for navigating the music business and life, but even more so he needed to believe in himself. He was striving to get a slice of the business on his own terms.

We talked almost daily for thirty years. How could I know it would be our last call on June 5, 2015? The voice was as familiar as my own. "Hey, pimp, what's happnin'?" He was leaving for a performance in Las Vegas and told me, "I'll talk to ya when I get back." En route to the airport, Ron had a heart attack and died. To this day and probably for the rest of my life, I can't think or speak of him without tears. My dear brother, your favorite Spinners song was "I'll Be Around." That says it all.

Josh Sulfaro—Guitarist, singer, songwriter, composer, arranger

We met in the early 1990s through Dan Oestrike who was the bass player with the James Michael Simmons Band, a country music band formed by Josh and his brother Abe using their middle names and the maternal family surname. Josh is a *cat who can use his distinct bluegrass moan in a melancholy rockabilly or blues number, continue straight into a full-throated, edgy rock tune followed by a soft, mellow ballad while playing lead guitar throughout. When Josh plays, you immediately know it's him—a signature style, unpretentious and natural with a born-to-do-it aura. He also plays flamenco guitar.

Josh is the brother of the late Detroit musician, author and poet Abe Sulfaro (1970-2014), both brothers multi-genre artists and graduates of the jazz-based, renowned Berklee College of Music in Boston. Returning home to the Detroit area after college, they were aware that at the time they probably couldn't make a living playing live rock, but the new country movement was in full swing. Using multi-genre reach, they founded the James Michael Simmons Band, Detroit's best known and widely followed country group during the early '90s. The brothers knew how to build a following and how to negotiate with live music venues. They became music chameleons, later founding Champion Eternal (hard rock originals) and Brother, Inc. (pop, R&B and easy listening tunes for the casinos). When they auditioned at one Detroit casino, it became apparent that the committee was expecting Black performers, probably because of the duo's name, Brother, Inc. Reading disappointment on the faces of the committee, the "brothers" broke into a Marvin Gaye tune and were hired on the spot.

Josh is a nomad geographically and musically. He went on to study flamenco guitar in Spain and relocated to Los Angeles and later Nashville. He has composed catalogs of music.

Josh Sulfaro on stage in Nashville TN

He laid down his guitar a couple of years ago for reasons that include performance fatigue, feeling he was on a dead-end street with the recording industry in the United States, and the death of his brother from pancreatic cancer in 2014. Josh currently lives in Italy part of each year. Once in a while, he does shows with Nashville artists. It's okay, Josh. There are reasons and seasons.

Dr. Luis ("Dr. Louie") Torregrosa—Jazz scholar

Skip Gildersleeve introduced me to Dr. Louie. Like me, he's a purist. In a record store, we're like crack addicts, giddy and short of breath. Louie is a collector extraordinaire with more than 17,000 titles in his collection.

I'm enamored of this jazz scholar. So many music journalists and interviewers lack Dr. Louie's academic depth, merely skimming the surface. They don't deep dive because they haven't done the research and are unable to ask questions that yield insightful answers. They can't produce a beneath-the-surface look into the artist or the music. It's too often the case that great historians exist outside the public lens. I'm not certain he'd even be interested, but Luis should write a column, reviews or a book. He definitely should do podcasts.

Beyond our mutual interest in jazz, Dr. Louie always encourages me. He's a counselor who graciously analyzes and discusses options with me. I look forward to his visits when we drink and watch jazz videos and documentaries. There are few people with whom I can have the depth of conversation about jazz that I can have with this dear friend and colleague.

Johnny Trudell—Trumpeter, orchestra leader, composer, arranger

In the mid-1970s, I began checking out performers that included Tony Bennett, Della Reese, Lou Rawls, Jose' Feliciano and Billy Eckstine at *DB's Club in Dearborn, all backed by the Johnny

Trudell Orchestra. I respected Johnny's work from the Motown era, especially his great horn arrangements, and his orchestra was made up of the best Detroit musicians. Johnny would come to my table and talk, and he understood how important music was to me. One evening, he asked if I'd be interested in sitting in with the orchestra. Of course I would!

Even though I wasn't a regular in his group, Johnny believed in me and coaxed me to progress, encouraging me to look at music from an academic perspective. I believe he was trying to groom me, and I didn't take that as seriously as I should have. Johnny included me and my bands in events such as the Michigan Jazz Festival. He's a mentor who gave me opportunities to play with top-notch *cats, among the best in the country, and provided some of the best stage experiences of my life. The Trudell family is dear to me. Johnny's son Jeff, a drummer, performed on some of my recordings. To this day, Johnny still plays. He's one of the finest trumpet players I've ever heard.

Walter White—Trumpeter, composer, arranger, producer

We met through saxophonist Rick Margitza in 1980. Walter has a resume that is world class, having played with Maynard Ferguson, conductor Dave Matthews, Dave Holland, Bob James, the Mingus Band (Charles Mingus) and Wynton Marsalis. Walter has formed his own big bands and appears on many records, movie sound tracks and music for TV. He's also a classical musician and has played with symphony orchestras all over the country.

Walter understands me, and we've had enjoyable times on a personal basis as well as working together. He made *Dan Lewis & Friends performances and recordings come to life, bumping us up to a higher level by incorporating beautifully arranged horn parts. He knows how to fuse rock and jazz. Walter never side-steps anything, and he doesn't let sleeping dogs lie. He has no problem telling you the truth, so you'd better be able to handle it. I like his outspoken approach and always take his advice because I can feel that he has my best interest at heart. Walter leaves any music situation better than he found it, and the musicians he's involved with are better off, too. At this writing, he's putting an album together, a compilation of his compositions for big band. These days, I don't see Walter as much as I used to, but I think of him often.

CHAPTER FOURTEEN
Morphing the Molecules

Music gives a soul to the universe, wings to the mind,
flight to the imagination, and life to everything.

Plato

Bach is how buildings got taller. It's how we got to the moon.

Charles Mingus

Music is powerful juju. In Coltrane's track "Ascension" (album *Ascension*), his solo is strong, changing over time, playing out into the universe with total freedom. You want to surrender and go there, traveling outside yourself without limits...upward...altering your awareness like meditation. There are also moments of deep human connection that elevate us and leave us forever changed.

Transported

The doorbell rings and I hear Mom greeting someone. The voice is familiar, guitarist and songwriter Josh Sulfaro. We talk for a while, catching up on each others' lives, and Mom makes lunch for us. Our conversation continues about playing for live audiences. We compare American and European audiences, noting how Americans want what they want and know how they want it served up, whereas Europeans are more likely to attend a live performance to experience the art and the artist.

Josh and his brother, Abe, have been making a living playing country music, but the repetition and singular sound are frustrating and unfulfilling. When you play within a genre, you're placed in a labelled box. The venue and audience buy a certain flavor, and that's what they expect. Venturing outside the labelled box can cause audience dissatisfaction. Remaining in the box is exhausting, leads to performer burnout, and can wall the performer off from an audience. It places borders around the interaction and eliminates any surprise in hearing something new and different. Either people don't appreciate variation in art forms, or they don't want them mixed together. Once you face that reality, you either have to accept it for what it is and carry on (languish artistically) or make tough choices. Josh is contemplating those choices and has come here to commiserate with a brother.

When there's a guest at my house, it's a simple choice. You either talk or you listen to music but not both. Having solved the problems of the music business, Josh and I put on some jazz, John Patitucci's *Another World*, a fitting title for what happens as we listen. I turn it up—loud—allowing nothing but the music to engulf us. During our undisturbed listening, the surroundings are suspended and there's a lightness of my body, almost a sense of levitating. When the music stops, we discover this was a mutual experience. It's a memorable early '90s visit by a brother and an unforgettable departure from here and now.

The impact of music varies. Sometimes it sneaks up on you, opens a portal, abducts you and floats you around in another dimension.

Indelible Moments

Like so many experiences, I owe this night in 1994 to Larry Fratangelo. I've accompanied him to a dinner party attended by notables including dancer/choreographer/ singer/actor, Gregory Hines. Toward the end of the evening, Greg and I are talking about the old icons in dance: Bojangles Robinson, Peg Leg Bates, Arthur Duncan and Sammy Davis, Jr. It leads to a memorable discussion, one that remains forever with me, about how hard it can be to break into show business, especially for Blacks in the early days, all the way back to vaudeville. Greg is from that lineage (Hines, Hines & Dad) and spent his early years dancing at the Apollo. We speak of film historian and author Donald Bogle. We talk about Ethel Waters, "Amos 'n Andy" (created by two White guys) and Lena Horne. I listen as Greg recounts history and pays homage to those who preceded him.

When a master is willing to share experiences and wisdom, I tune in. Like when I was given a brief time with Alice Coltrane, Kenny Garrett and Pat Metheny, this evening with Greg Hines reminds me that I shouldn't miss an opportunity to shut up and listen because these are moments I'll never have again. I'm absorbing Greg's words, but more importantly I'm discerning his deeper meaning. He must be reading it in my eyes and my voice—passion, determination and a desire to perform. He says, "If you know you're good, don't take 'no' for an answer." He shares his own experiences and relates stories about racial minority struggles that parallel my own. I'm told not to cheat myself, to nurture my gift. Greg also tells me what it takes to sustain a career. "After a few decades, even if you're legendary, you have to reinvent yourself in order to stay relevant because people who come along later don't know who you are. If you're lucky, lightning will strike again and again."

We talk so late into the evening that Larry leaves without me. Greg and I have gotten inside each other's sensibilities tonight. What he has shared is relevant to my life and leaves me with much to think about, particularly not counting myself out and the concept of self-reinvention, another way of looking at morphing the molecules. Here I am writing this book. Lightning strikes.

Behind the Mask

> **It is an absolute human certainty that no one can know his own beauty or perceive a sense of his own worth until it has been reflected back to him in the mirror of another loving, caring human being.**
>
> *John Joseph Powell*

Larry Fratangelo and I are in Anaheim, California for the 1982 NAMM (National Association of Music Merchants) show. We decide to go to the *China Club, a place where stars hang out. Larry is mingling, walking around to check the place out, so I'm sitting alone. None other than Sam Kinison walks up to my table. "Hi, I'm Sam. Do you mind if I sit?" Of course I recognize him immediately and invite him to join me.

For some reason that I'm about to discover, Sam begins a personal dialogue, sharing his story and asking about mine. Because I've learned when to shut up and listen, Sam is permitted be himself. He's breaking ground in the entertainment world, locked into a contrived public persona. He's finding success with a comedic style—unabashedly loud, crude and in your face. The public expectation that famous people live their everyday lives "in character" diminishes their identity. I'd like to think Sam Kinison senses that I'll relate to him as a human being, not a caricature. As we talk, it becomes clear that he's battling this duality. He's grappling with an internal clash between his background and a desire to be a comedian, telling me he used to be a Pentecostal preacher, a role that doesn't square with his stage and film persona. Truth really can be stranger than fiction. He's hoping to reconcile opposing (or are they?) aspects of his personality and tells me, "You hope you've made the right choice. I have a different style as an entertainer and feel I can change the face of comedy." What he's really getting at is self-trust. People are walking past our table to get a close look, but they don't distract him.

Sam is gentle and kind. We laugh and talk and laugh and talk. As he's telling me about his family, Larry returns, unintentionally interrupting the flow of conversation between Sam and me. I introduce them and Sam says, "It's beautiful meeting you, Larry. Dan and I are having a delightful conversation, and we're not finished. I've got Dan. We'll find you, okay?" Classic Kinison, not even subtle. He's telling Larry to get lost for a while longer.

During our brief time together, this gentle soul touches me on a deep level. These moments contain one of the warmest, most pleasant conversations I've ever had. There's freedom when the phony veneer can disappear and the barriers are removed. Sam is reaching out, seeking self-actualization, and his love for humanity penetrates my consciousness.

There's a story of Sam's tragic death following an auto accident. He appeared to be talking to an unseen presence, at first telling the invisible someone he didn't want to go, then pausing to listen and answering peacefully, "Okay, okay, okay." Sam yielded during his negotiation with a higher power. This is why I revere the metaphysical dimension. We're never really gone, just transitioning.

Afterword

In many ways, my physical condition has created the circumstances that have made my life a rich tapestry of talented people, artistic energies, memorable happenings and unforgettable places. A disability like cerebral palsy fogs up the window into situations and relationships, making it difficult to discern whether acceptance as a performing musician is acceptance for the right reasons. The foremost right reason is solid musicianship and the value it brings to any piece of music, band or performer. It has often occurred to me that my friendships with well known musicians might not have happened if I walked around like others. My skill as a percussionist is more than adequate. But are the artists who have befriended me, performed with me, and taken the time and effort to lift and transport me simply caring people? Has it merely been out of empathy? In some cases, it's not clear and I'll always wonder. In other cases, I know beyond any doubt that they're artists who have recognized my passion and musicianship.

Throughout my life, the power switch in my brain has been stuck in the "on" position. My mind and my body are frustrated cohorts because I've never been one to settle for daydreaming, pretending or being a spectator. I want to really fly the kite, but that's becoming more and more difficult as the years pass. Aging is literally a sore subject. As I've aged, the aches and pains have become greater, so I try not to focus on them. The last decade has kicked my ass. Too often my mind says "yes," but my body grumbles "no." When I was younger, I had a higher tolerance for discomfort and could readily shift my weight from one skinny buttock to the other to relieve the constant ache in my tailbone from sitting in a wheelchair.

Music has always been my beautiful air balloon, transporting me outside my body. The greatest moments of escape have been on stage where there's a lowered perception of pain and an electromagnetic pull toward the audience...followed by a sobering comedown to the ever-present intersection of psychological and physical pain. I prefer to get through the day having spent minimal time on bodily requirements and maintenance, not only because they involve discomfort but also because they necessitate the physical assistance of others. At the time of this writing, I'm recovering from a fractured tibia. Today my tolerance is being tested by a visiting nurse who's taking my blood pressure and asking irritating questions. Please just put me unrestrained in the back of a van and drive it over a cliff.

Worse than the physical discomfort are the times when I struggle to reconcile the current world of musicians with a personal perspective. I'm from a generation that learned everything organically—on the front lines in smoky clubs. I'm not diggin' the millennial way nor am I feeling like reinventing myself to accommodate generational differences. Where music is involved, I'm Clint Eastwood in the movie *Gran Torino* yelling, "Get off my lawn!" It seems to me that I've lived through hard times that were the best of times. I've become the old guy who says, "Back in my day, things were cool." Most tunes now are short lived, but I guess it's all "compared to what?" Looking back over my life, comparing the way things were with the way things are now, I wouldn't be completely honest if I didn't admit that I consider much of pop culture, with some exceptions, to be kitsch, a shallow pond that will dry up.

I was afforded simpler times that younger musicians haven't known, times that provided freedoms and opportunities that don't exist now. Rock, jazz and blues were simpler, performed live in smaller venues with fewer barriers thrown up by a music industrial complex. People could get closer to the artist then. Musicians could reach their audiences with less pressure from a production line that leads to short-lived careers performing prototype tunes. My fondest hope now is for a market driven by and for the artists who create the music.

Musicians 15 to 45 can't be expected to know what I know, but it does seem that they might thirst a bit more for historical context...and not just where music is concerned. The world has changed and is continuing to change. I don't expect younger musicians to conform to history to the extent that it limits them to a narrow lane. I'm not holding a sign with an arrow that says, "This Way," but I'm not exactly comfortable with the state of the art, either. Rather than mellowing, I ponder the new templates and wonder if I've lived beyond relevance.

There are new voices and new styles with powerful words heard in the rap/hip hop genre. It's poetry, some of it making impactful social and political observations and statements. I'm certainly not put off by those statements. In fact, I value them. They're the human spirit and democracy set to music and prose. It's a not a new phenomenon. Buttressed by music that mirrored inequities and injustice during the beat generation of the 1950s and the folk revival of the 1960s, social and cultural change took place. Where my embrace of the current trends ends is the pervasive lack of interest in origins and history. Just like everything else in life, one needs a foundation on which to build understanding and skills in music. It's all connected like Roy Brooks' percussion, reverberating African rhythms that have existed for millennia. Awareness of where your music began and how it evolved deepens your understanding and enhances the entire experience as well as the art.

Musicians used to spend time mastering their instruments, now too often replaced by beat boxes and electronic, computer-generated rhythm tracks. Few musicians practice scales. They jump into music careers without investing the foundational work, considering themselves musicians and songwriters through the use of synthesizers. You can't create Roy Brooks' percussion this way because there's no hands-on or spiritual connection. I hold the belief that the study of music and relentless practice on one's instrument provide the foundations that lead to mastery. No cruising on a skateboard before learning to walk. I'm scared because we're now into the second and third generations of shortcuts, complacency and ignorance of origins. The implications go beyond music.

My son's a painter. All through school his teachers tell him he's a genius. I tell him to paint me a picture of an apple that looks like an apple before he paints me one that doesn't.
Go where you can go, but start from someplace recognizable.
                                                          Charles Mingus

The value and appreciation of art in general, that which enriches and elevates a culture, is being eroded by an illogical disdain for learning. It's as if there's a grievance against it—willful ignorance—some saying they've been turned off by academic elitism. Science is being pushed aside and even discredited, possibly at our peril. There's ideological push 'n shove. I observe this as someone who was unable to pursue higher education using the traditional path, so I've used other methods to learn all I could. Knowledge places the entire world and humanity within a broader context. More people should pick up a book and contemplate the information and concepts therein. What I'm saying isn't a judgment about intelligence or aptitude, and it doesn't flow from academic elitism because I could never fit into that world. The number of people who are content to live without intellectual growth is regressive and dangerous.

I have an unrequited desire to perform. It's not that I haven't had my days on stage but rather that I haven't performed as frequently as I've desired, as a lifestyle. People whom I haven't seen in years ask, "Are you still a musician?' When I tell them that I am, they say, "Still, huh?" These questions get under my skin because of their implications. Read between the lines. At the risk of sounding overly sensitive, it feels like they're implying that I'm forever treading water or that being a musician isn't a totally legit profession. Poor Dan, he must be slow in realizing it. I wonder if they think a musician's path is like climbing a regular career ladder, the less talented ones being stuck in place, gigging for dollars. After a lifetime in music, I can honestly say there are loose correlations between talent, commercial success, and fame as observed by drummer Andy Newmark (Chapter 4: Elusive Expectations). Unless they've lived a musician's life, people who work regular jobs have no clue what it takes to become a musician or what it means to be one. They seem to think you'd have become a big star if you were talented enough or that by now you surely must have concluded that music is just an enjoyable pastime, something you do in addition to a real job. Having their initial questions answered about what I'm up to these days, well meaning people move on to a superficial smile and trite remarks like "You must be having a great time" or "It sounds like fun!" "Great time" and "fun" are hardly the words for the serious pursuit of music. I'm not exactly snowboarding or taking day trips to theme parks. Can't they say, "It must be fulfilling to do what you love?" I'd be good with that.

I used to think I was invincible. At 63 years of age, I ponder mortality as I look back at happenings and circumstances, framing them in degrees of my own relative madness at the time. It allows for contrast against whatever factors might have been at play, and it's why I look sideways at people who wear rose-colored glasses and those who say they have no regrets. There's a malcontent trapped inside this body. I didn't choose happy, smiley types to perform with me, either. Life is full of struggles, and I'm sad more often than not.

As with any passion, music as a career brings as many disappointments as it brings moments of enjoyment and elation. I believe in music in a spiritual sense and in helping others as they've helped me, leaving people and circumstances better than they were when I found them. It's a purpose in and of itself, a soulful quest. Music and other natural gifts are not ours to covet. They're for sharing like the neighborhood kid, now in his early 60s, tried to do with music on a transistor radio. I kick down the door if that's what it takes to pursue dreams and to share what's meant to be shared. It's exhausting, but I'll soar peacefully later.

I realize now more than ever that music saved my life and has sustained me. It was there for a child who sought escape, joy and refuge, a child who like Coltrane wanted to share the gift of music with the world. Thanks to music, I bypassed the growing pains and the awkward, self-conscious days of adolescence because I was adopted by *cats older than I. For the most part, I've lived outside the mainstream, inspired and made whole by music.

I think the main thing a musician would like to do is give a picture to the listener of the many wonderful things that he knows of and senses in the universe...That's what I would like to do. I think that's one of the greatest things you can do in life and we all try to do it in some way. The musician's is through his music.
John Coltrane

♫

The writing of this story has given me many opportunities to recall my upbringing with love, gratitude and respect for Chuck and Suzanne Lewis, two imperfect and mismatched people. What they did for me was perfect under the most imperfect circumstances. I inherited the best of each of them. Nothing was just handed to me because of my birth condition. Dad, you gave me a firm grip on reality and consequences. You continue to be the loving tough guy in my heart. Mom, you will always reside in my most tender memories, not only your love and care but also the joyful, entertaining moments when you danced like Mick Jagger and your fondness for the Beatles and Greg Allman. Looking back now, I realize how precious those moments were. In my heart and mind, you're selfless, packing my gear into cabs that took me to music venues, baking cookies to get the neighborhood kids to come inside and listen to music with me, and above all supporting my dreams and sharing my consciousness. I'll keep on for both of you for the rest of my time here.

Beyond all this, I'm going to evolve into an exotic talking bird, one that has rhythm.

Dan Lewis

Homage

These people occupy special places in my heart. They've been on this journey with me for many years, enriching my life. Some of them have been present at intersections, some in episodes and others with each sunset. There's good karma in our shared experiences and our bonds.

- Judy Adams, Detroit radio personality

  I'm grateful for the exposure you gave *Dan Lewis & Friends from 1976 into the 1990s. You're an innovator and a multi-genre groundbreaker who played our demos and gave me interviews on WDET-FM, one of the best radio stations in the country.

- Pistol Allen (1932-2002), drummer

- Jerome & Jimmy Ali, a.k.a. The Brothers Ali, jazz and R&B musicians

- Becky Anderson

  Thanks for sharing hang out time with me over the years.

- Ralphe Armstrong, bassist

  You make the bass sing, as demanding as lead guitar. Thank you, Ralphe, for your interest in my projects.

- Marcus Belgrave (1936-2015), jazz trumpeter

- Norma Bell, saxophonist/singer/producer

  We met in 1976 through Lyman Woodard. You always valued my opinion and auditioned the musicians I referred to you. Thank you for some great times and allowing me to sit in with Norma Jean Bell & the All Stars at *Axels.

- Larry Benjamin, promoter and Parliament-Funkadelic's road manager

  We met through Russ Gibb at the *Grande Ballroom in 1968. You invited me to parties at your apartment in the Clarkston Towers in Northland where I got to meet music greats.

- George Bennett (1951-2021), drummer, and family

- George Benson (1929-2019), jazz alto and tenor saxophonist/educator (Henry Ford Community College).

  I was given educational opportunities when you allowed me to sit in on your music theory classes. You broke it down so that even a dyslexic guy could get it. I otherwise wouldn't have been exposed to these chosen academics, especially what I learned about fearlessness and improvisational responsibility. You always made room if I wanted to drop in.

- Bess Bonnier (1928-2011), jazz pianist / composer / educator

- Kern Brantley, bassist

  We met around 1979 through Ron Smith (The Spinners). Your talent led you to Janet Jackson and more recently Lady Gaga. You were there when we played that ill-advised prom on Grosse Ile years ago, always willing to help out when asked. I'm proud to know you.

- Randy Brecker, trumpeter/flugelhornist/composer
- Doug Brown, keyboardist/composer/arranger/producer/songwriter/singer
- Robert Bruce, guitarist/keyboardist/singer/composer/arranger/producer/songwriter
- Buddy Budson, jazz pianist/composer/arranger
- Hiram Bullock (1955-2008), jazz funk and fusion guitarist

  You were always willing to help out and play when I needed you.

- Paul Butterfield Blues Band members George Davidson (drummer), Rod Hicks (bass, backing and lead vocals), Gene Dinwiddie (saxophone, flute, backing vocals), Teddy Harris, Jr. (keyboards, piano) and David Sanborn (saxophone, percussion)

- Dan Carlisle, radio personality and DJ at Michigan State University, WXYZ, WRIF and WKNR.

  We met in 1973. Thanks for the invitations to visit your station when you were spinning. We have so much in common musically.

- James Carter, jazz trumpeter

  We met in 1980 when you were doing performances with Leonard King's Strata Nova Orchestra and you were preparing to attend Blue Lake Music Conservatory. You borrowed my Coltrane records, and I got to know your parents—cherished memories. You're one of the first world class trumpeters I ever heard.

- Regina Carter, jazz violinist

  We met in 1980 through Leonard King when you were with his Strata Nova Orchestra. We talked on hot summer days when you told me about studying and about coming upon your own "voice" with your instrument. Thank you for the encouragement.

- Chris Collins, saxophonist/jazz educator (Wayne State University)/composer/arranger/Artistic Director of the Detroit Jazz Festival

  We met through Mark Moultrup in 1990. I've never enjoyed playing with anyone more than with you, Chris, so similar to Michael Brecker with great cascading and soloing. You're an anchor in any ensemble, lyrical and abstract, and yet you bring it home.

- Michael Colone, producer/composer/singer/songwriter/ guitarist

- Ron Colone, writer/performer/music historian/concert promoter

- Danny Colton, bassist

  We met through Gary Schunk in 1979. Without a doubt, you're one of the best bassists anywhere, playing quietly with such execution, everything strategically placed, making musical sense. Your solos are melodious, taking the listener with you. You arrange bass parts to lift the music up and have mastered the art of soloing over jazz changes. Impeccable.

- Conti Family, steadfast

- Kenny Cox (1940-2008), pianist/composer

  We met through Danny Spencer in 1977. I appreciate how supportive you were, recognizing my dexterity in spite of the physical challenges and telling me, "You have a gift. I've never seen someone as determined as you are. When you play, you enhance. Thank you, Kenny.

- Hubie Crawford (died 2007), bassist

- Maureen Daley, publicist for *Dan Lewis & Friends

- Jack Dryden, bassist

  You and I met through Gary Schunk in the early '90s, and then you joined *Dan Lewis & Friends. You "got" the vision for a big band, giving pop a bigger voice in jazz format, and helped me accomplish just that. You've been solid through-out the years, always there for me, truthful and open, traits that led to mutual respect. I dig your intellect as well as your musicianship. I admire your understanding of hip, no wanna-be cool jive. We've shared an escapade or two, so when I think of you, Jack, I think of joy and laughter.

- Jim Dulzo of WEMU (Eastern Michigan University) Radio, writer for the Detroit News and Director of the Montreux-Detroit Jazz Festival (now the Detroit Jazz Festival).

  You made my dream for Dan Lewis & Friends come true. We talked ideas, you listened, you always returned my calls and you made time to meet with me. You put *Dan Lewis & Friends on the stage at the Montreux-Detroit Jazz Fest and allowed me to add specials guests Dave Liebman and Rick Margitza. In doing so, you gave me one of the greatest performance experiences of my life and an opportunity to become part of something greater than myself.

- Ron English, jazz guitarist
- Bill Evans, jazz saxophonist/composer

Thank you for your timely responses to my requests. You were never too busy to lend support.

- Janice Frankel, American standards and Brazilian singer
- Pat Freer, drummer/composer
- Jim Gallert, "Jazzlogy" jazz historian/writer

We met at WDET about thirty years ago, and you were a breath of fresh air. I'm in awe of your scholarly approach to research and writing. I've read lots of books on music but none as substantive as *Before Motown: A History of Jazz in Detroit 1920-1960* by Lars Bjorn with Jim Gallert, University of Michigan Press. You've always shown interest in my projects. Thank you, Jim, for understanding that music is my life.

- Dennis and Nancy Gibbons, dear friends for many years
- Mike and Judy Gilbert, dear friends for many years
- Skip Gildersleeve (1957-2013), sound engineer, guitar tech and road crew member for Rush, Bob Seger and Steely Dan
- Billy Harper, tenor saxophonist and Blue Note legend from New York City.

I pushed to get you booked at the *Montreux-Detroit Jazz Festival (now the Detroit Jazz Festival) when promoters were tending to schedule the same performers year after year.

- Perry Hughes, guitarist

  We met at *Baker's Keyboard Lounge around 1979 when you and Larry Fratangelo were playing with Earl Klugh. You're one of Detroit's finest guitarists, a George Benson fave, always your own man no matter what big deal cats you play with. You're a world class cat, and yet content wherever you are—an extraordinary, gentle, laid-back soul. You're also a sage, so a person had better be prepared for the truth if he asks for your opinion. You once told me, "The problem is only as big as you want it to be." You continue to play at Baker's, cascading through solos...unpretentious. Like you told me, "You know, Dan, I came here to play."

- Ali Muhammad Jackson, Jr., jazz bassist

- Lamont Johnson, bassist

  We met in 1979 when you were playing at London Bridge with a group called Brainstorm. Wow, the epitome of bass players! You're a pro with business acumen who emphasized to me the importance of being my own boss because club owners have their own agendas. You taught me to never give up personal power and that I need to make a decision about whether or not to pursue an opportunity if I can't be in control. You embody the meaning of entrepreneur with endeavors of your own choosing.

- Mike Joyce, bassist

- Marvin Kahn (1918-2005), pianist

- Mark Kieme, reed instrumentalist extraordinaire and educator (Oakland University, Rochester, Michigan)

- Ron Kischuk, trombonist
- Earl Klugh, guitarist/composer
- Joe LoDuca, film score composer

  I'm so glad to have met you through Larry Fratangelo in 1978 when you were in the band Cordova. From you I learned about improvisation, freedom outside self through beautiful melodies, and how to trust myself and let the music speak. I have the utmost respect for you as a world class cat.

- Jim and Debbie Lusk, dear friends
- Bob, Margaret and Colleen Lusk, dear friends
- Rick Margitza, saxophonist
- Michael Marsac, guitarist/vocalist/songwriter
- Don Mayberry (1951-2011), acoustic bassist

  We met in 1977 when I was with Johnny Trudell at the Hyatt Regency DB's Club in Dearborn. You let me know when I was taking life too seriously, keeping me plugged into reality but also encouraging me. You brought me back to earth. No patronizing. Thanks, Don, for lunches at your house and time spent in your garden as we talked.

- Dan McCann, drummer
- Chris McKee, singer
- Al McKenzie (deceased), pianist and Temptations Music Director

  We met through Johnny Trudell. Your resume' is packed with Motown history. You brought a funky jazz twist, elevating the sounds of Motown groups. You were an educator and mentor who helped musicians realize their self-worth. You told me, "You don't have to compromise your style even when you're playing someone else's music. We're onto something, aren't we?" When talking about recording, you said, "It doesn't matter when you do it or how long it takes as long as you get it done. When you're gone, it stands forever, a document of your legacy."

- Gayelynn McKinney, drummer

  We met at the 1982 Montreux-Detroit Jazz Festival (now the Detroit Jazz Festival). You're the proud legacy of your uncles, Ray and Harold. You're also living proof of the physical capacity of women, especially considering the muscle power and endurance required of a drummer. When a woman plays drums, something special happens! You pulse a rhythm section forward with straight-ahead playing and sophisticated time signatures.

- Dave McMurray, saxophonist
- Ali Francisco Mora, now widely known as Francisco Mora, jazz drummer/composer/educator
- Shaun Murphy, blues and R&B singer
- Michael G. Nastos, WEMU radio broadcaster and music historian
- Mark and Marcia Navarre, dear friends
- Helen Nolan, dear friend
- Skip Norris (1959-2017), jazz advocate/promoter/event manager and booking agent

- Larry Nozero (1934-2005)

  I met you in the '70s through Johnny Trudell. Thank you for your memorable stories from the road and about working with greats including Henry Mancini. You told me not to go into music thinking about money but rather for the music itself, to devote my life to it. You told me to listen to my inner muse, and your advice didn't fall on deaf ears.

- Tim O'Brien, friend

- Huel Perkins, WJBK news anchor

  You gave *Dan Lewis & Friends invaluable coverage and promotions that packed the venues where we played.

- Scott Peterson, a.k.a. "E Dog" (died 2011), saxophonist

- Ray Portugal, percussionist/multi-instrumentalist

- Bernard Purdie, multi-genre drummer

- Larry and Nancy Reaume and Family, dear friends

  Talk about catnip for this cat! You owned a music store in Riverview where I spent endless hours. After many years in the downriver Detroit area, you moved to Los Angeles to escape the Michigan weather, giving me a place to stay when I visited L.A. You believed in me, supported my aspirations, and your family transported me to meetings and music venues. I'm forever grateful.

- David Reinstein, saxophonist/pianist/composer/sound designer/hybrid jazz artist

  I used to go to *Baker's to hear you when you were with a band called Orange Lake Drive. You're an intellectual cat who challenges the norms in music, religion, politics, philosophy and human existence. You ask my views and debate them with me. When I go dark, you challenge me openly but without judgment. We've played well together because it's another way to communicate ideas. You've shown me other ways of thinking with your frequent question "Why?" With you, I don't get away with loose, shaky concepts, but any topic is open to discussion. You're an artist, a seeker and a protector.

- Luis Resto, multi-instrumentalist/songwriter/record producer
- Mario Resto, performer/songwriter/composer/producer
- Tony Robertson, drummer
- Ernie Rodgers (1934-2014), saxophonist/educator at Detroit Public Schools and Wayne State University
- Alex Rogalski, Brazilian guitarist
- Mike Sawicki, drummer
- Rick Sawicki, drummer
- Walt Sczymanski, trumpeter
- Dennis Sheridan, percussionist

  Your encouragement and the energy you bring to music are very much appreciated. You try new things and trust yourself, and in doing so, you taught me to do the same. Lots of ideas were summoned forth with your input in the studio with Larry Fratangelo's Drum Devils.

- Jim Simonson, bassist
- John Slitti, percussionist

- Chad Smith of the Red Hot Chili Peppers

  We first met in 1988 when Larry Fratangelo was working with the band Pharaoh and I was invited to rehearsals. With you, Chad, music comes first. You're a go-getter with the ability to focus and remain in the moment. In spite of your success, you're gracious and humble, and I admire you as a human being.

- Larry Smith, saxophonist

- Bobbie Smith (1936-2013) of The Spinners

- R.J. Spangler, jazz, blues and R & B drummer/producer/promoter

- Derek St. Holmes, guitarist/vocalist

- Danny Spencer, drummer

  We met in 1979 when you were with a band called Mixed Bag. You're one of the finest bebop drummers I've ever heard—firebrand drumming, brute force, a tornado. In your relentless way, you raise the level of connections within compositions. When you and Gary Schunk team up, other musicians had better be up to the task or get mowed over.

- Tom Starr, drummer

  We met in 1986 through Gary Schunk. You've always been a pleasure to work with, supportive and keeping me informed about what you're doing. Thank you for the encouragement during *Dan Lewis & Friends. You're always positive—pleasure, never pressure.

- The Stockwell Brothers, guitarists/singers/songwriters

- Stacy Stowell, dear friend

- Mark and Ann Sturgis, dear friends

- Tony Suhy, bassist

- Abe Sulfaro (1970-2014), vocalist/keyboardist/guitarist/music productions engineer/songwriter/author

  Thank you for sharing a legacy in writing, some of it included in this autobiography. I met you and your brother Josh (guitarist/singer/songwriter/composer) through Dan Oestrike when you were playing the Detroit country circuit in the '90s. Perhaps because of your background at Berklee College of Music, you guys could play it all—jazz, R&B, rock, pop—not painted into any corner. Thanks for looking out for me when I was almost abducted by a sicko (Chapter 6, section "Saved by the Band"). You saved my ass! You are deeply missed. Rest well, brother.

- Danny Taylor, keyboardist/vocalist/songwriter

- Joel Taylor, son of Danny Taylor (above), close friend and confidant

- Tim Teal, guitarist

- Professor Dennis Tini, jazz pianist and faculty at Wayne State University Music Department from 1973 to 2015 (42 years)

  You showed selfless interest in the advancement of those you taught and mentored.

- Bob Tye, guitarist with the Detroit Symphony Orchestra and within the Detroit jazz community

  When I sought your input for *Dan Lewis & Friends, you helped me realize that I can play what I love with integrity and still give the music commercial appeal. You also let me know when I was off track and taught me there's more than one way to deliver.

- Skeeto Valdez, drummer/percussionist/instructor

- Earl Van Dyke (1930-1992), pianist

  We met in 1981 through Don Mayberry. You're legendary, on so many Motown hits. You led me to appreciate the Great American Songbook and composers such as Alec Wilder and George Gershwin. You showed me that a tune can be a vehicle, that in an arranger's hands, a song can come to life or become a jazz interpretation.

- Skip Van Winkle (1944-2018) of the early 1970s duo Teegarden & Van Winkle, later the Skip Van Winkle Band

  You were one of the finest Hammond B-3 players I ever heard and the person who got me interested in astrology.

- Keith Vreeland (1938-2018), jazz pianist

- Ursula Walker, jazz singer

- Rodney Whitaker, double bassist/educator

- Buster Williams, double bassist/composer/bandleader

- Tony Williams (1945-1997), jazz drummer extraordinaire

  Thank you, brother, for so many calls to check on me and invite me to hear you play, for putting me on your list at *Baker's, and for encouraging me when I was forming *Dan Lewis & Friends.

- Lyman Woodard (1942-2009), jazz organist/pianist/composer/band leader

  We met through Leonard King. You're a Detroit legend and one of the finest Hammond B-3 players I've ever heard, in a class with John Patton, Charles Earland and Jack McDuff. We shared a love of the poetry of Charles Bukowski, the writing of William Burroughs, old R&B records and vintage black and white movies.

- Belita Woods (1948-2012), singer with Parliament-Funkadelic for two decades

- Bernie (1944-2016) and Judy Worrell, dear friends. Bernie was a keyboardist, record producer and a founding member of Parliament-Funkadelic.

- Linda Yohn, host of "The Swing Set," WRCJ-FM

You know how to cut through barriers experienced by artists in the jazz scene. As a well known and respected radio personality who spent 30 years (1987-2017) as music director at WEMU (NPR jazz station at Eastern Michigan University), Detroit musicians appreciate your kind support, Linda. You were genuinely interested and supported *Dan Lewis & Friends, inviting me to be a guest on your program a couple of times. I felt embraced by you in a city that too often doesn't value and recognize its own. You boosted attendance at my gigs in venues where, if fill seats weren't filled, the musicians weren't invited back. Forever grateful, Linda.

- Vincent York, jazz saxophonist/bandleader/educator

- Alexander Zonjic, flutist

We met at *Baker's Keyboard Lounge around 1979. Thank you for many bookings of *Dan Lewis & Friends at festivals. You've taught me how to take charge of my own situation. You've also taught me that a musician must know all aspects of the business and that if you know what you want, you can get what you need. You're an impresario and one of the most masterful businessmen in the D. I'm proud to call you my friend, and I'm forever grateful for so much solid advice over the years.

INDEX

- Alvin's

  Hangout, nightclub, deli and music venue located at the upper end of Detroit's *Cass Corridor. Its heyday was the 1970s, later becoming a popular music venue in the 1980s and 1990s. Then Midtown heated up far to the south of Alvin's, and it became as likely to be closed as it was to be open. It later became Tony V's Tavern.

- Americana Hotel

  Opened in 1962 with 2,000 rooms, the first New York City hotel with over 1,000 rooms since the Waldorf Astoria in 1931. It became the Sheraton New York Times Hotel, a 51-story structure and one of the world's 100 tallest hotels. It is located at 811 Seventh Avenue in Midtown.

- American Songbook

  Collectively, the most influential American popular music and jazz standards from the early twentieth century, also known as American Standards. It is not any particular book or list of songs but rather a loosely defined set of songs written for theater and film from the 1920s through the

1950s by composers such as George Gershwin, Cole Porter, Irving Berlin, Richard Rodgers, Jerome Kern, Harold Arlen and Johnny Mercer. There was a renewed interest in the standards by rock and pop singers in the 1970s.

- Axels

  Nightclub located at Nine Mile and Evergreen that hosted top Detroit R&B acts. It was open for several years during the early 1980s.

- Baker's Keyboard Lounge

  Known as the world's oldest jazz club, opening in 1934 and having an 86-year history. Most nationally known jazz musicians have played on Baker's stage. The 99-seat room is furnished in art deco and serves soul food. It's a performance venue for the finest Detroit musicians. Baker's is located at 20510 Livernois.

- Batá

  Nigerian sacred drums used for complex rhythms known as toques, corresponding with ceremonial phases. They are honored and celebrated as "talking drums" that communicate with dieties.

- Bembé

  An Afro-Cuban rhythm. The term also refers to the set of three Cuban drums of African ancestry on which the rhythm is played, the dancing that accompanies the rhythm and the celebration in which it is used. In Cuba, there are three distinct styles of Bembé.

- Bert's Marketplace

  Complex located in Detroit's Eastern Market at 2727 Russell Street. It contains four clubs: Jazz Room, Motown Room, Hasting Street Hall and the Warehouse Theater. Music genres include jazz, hip hop, R&B and blues.

- Blue Note

  Los Angeles-based jazz record label established by Alfred Lion and Max Margulis in 1939, deriving its name from the blue notes of jazz and blues. Originally dedicated to traditional jazz and small group swing, the label switched to recording modern jazz in 1947. Historically, Blue Note has been associated with hard bop but also recorded essential jazz albums in the avant-garde and free styles. More recently, the label has provided sampling tracks for hip hop artists.

- Bo-Mac's Lounge

  Bar-lounge on Gratiot Avenue with live jazz nights 1988-1992. The building has been demolished.

- Cascara

  A rhythm known as the "super power beat of Latin drummers." Cascara ("shell") takes its name from the shell of the timbale on which it is traditionally played. It is a complimentary rhythm to Son Clave. Cascara and Clave are interwoven, especially when played on different types of drums or percussion instruments.

- Cass Corridor

  Neighborhoods on the west end of Midtown Detroit along its main thoroughfare, Cass Avenue. In the 1960s and 1970s, the corridor was an area of cultural significance where artists rented cheap studio space. The artist community has produced a number of well known musicians and music groups including Sixto Rodriguez (a.k.a., Jesus Rodriguez, Rodriguez and "Sugarman" from the award-winning documentary about him) and White Stripes (Jack White/Third Man Records). The term was more commonly used prior to cultural erasure and displacement of residents. Cass Corridor has also been known as a poor neighborhood and an area plagued with drugs, violence and prostitution.

- cat

  1940s and 1950s hipster slang meaning a good musician. The term continues to be used when referring to a cool or respected jazz or blues musician. It has been hypothesized that the term cat is based on the smooth way jazz and blues musicians walk, talk, play and improvise. It's common "lingo" among musicians: "Man, those are some bad cats."

- Chelsea Hotel or Hotel Chelsea ("The Chelsea")

  250-unit, 12-story Queen Anne Revival/Victorian Gothic cooperative at 222 West 23rd Street between Seventh and Eighth Avenues. It was built between 1883 and 1885 in the Chelsea neighborhood of Manhattan. It has a grand staircase that extends the entire 12 floors. The hotel is the subject of five books, is mentioned in many songs, is a location in 11 films and is the subject of documentaries. Notable residents:

  ~Arthur C. Clarke wrote 2001: A Space Odyssey here.

~Allen Ginsberg and Gregory Corso used it as a place for philosophical and artistic exchange.

~Dylan Thomas died of pneumonia in room 205 in 1953.

~Nancy Spungen, girlfriend of Sid Vicious (Sex Pistols) was found stabbed to death here in 1972.

~Warhol superstars, a clique of New York City personalities promoted by the pop artist Andy Warhol in the 1960s and early 1970s, frequented and lived here.

~Many visual artists including Diego Rivera and Robert Maplethorpe (room 105 with Patti Smith, poet/author/singer/"punk poet laureate") stayed here.

~Musicians including Jim Morrison, Iggy Pop, Chick Corea, Jeff Beck, Dee Dee Ramone, Cher, Marianne Faithfull, Joni Mitchell, Bob Dylan, Alice Cooper, Jimi Hendrix, Canned Heat, Sid Vicious, Leonard Cohen, Janis Joplin, Madonna have stayed here.

The Chelsea no longer accepts long-term residents.

● The Chess Mate

Legendary 1960s Detroit folk coffeehouse and blues club located at the corner of Livernois and 6-Mile Road, growing out of the cultural around the University of Detroit. The owner, Morrie Widenbaum, was Michigan chess champion in 1963, and his original intent was for the club to be a place for serious chess players. The club has a history of late night concerts, cutting edge acts and iconic troubadours. It also has a rich and complicated history that includes James

Cotton who played harmonica in the middle of Livernois and a teen being shot by a gang known as the Errol Flynns. A wide range of artists that includes Neil Young, Linda Ronstadt, Joni Mitchell and the Blues Magoos honed their talent here. The venue is credited with introducing Detroit to disco during the 70s. The building later became the University Coin Laundry.

- Chess Records

  Chicago record company founded in 1950 by Leonard Chess (Rock and Roll Hall of Fame 1987), specializing in R&B and blues. Over the years, the label expanded into soul, gospel, early rock and roll and occasional jazz recordings. It was based at different south Chicago locations, the best known being 2120 South Michigan Avenue from 1957 to 1965, immortalized by the Rolling Stones in the instrumental "2120 South Michigan Avenue." The building is now the home of Willie Dixon's Blues Heaven Foundation. Iconic artists who recorded there include Muddy Waters, Etta James, Little Walter, Sonny Boy Williamson, John Lee Hooker, Bo Diddley, Wayne Cochran, Moms Mabley, Howlin' Wolf, Benny Goodman and Chuck Berry to name just a few. The company closed in 1975. Catastrophe occurred when the Chess building was sold. The new owners used chain saws to destroy over 250,000 abandoned vinyl records and disposed of them in a dumpster. The mass disposal of vinyl been called one of the music industry's most appalling events.

- China Club

  Los Angeles nightclub and legendary home of rock-star-packed Pro Jam, a gathering of cream-of-the-crop studio musicians and a venue for live music nights in Hollywood.

- Cinderella Ballroom

  Detroit theater built in 1924 on East Jefferson Avenue. The venue was one of the city's largest with almost 1,900 seats, built in Spanish Colonial style with a white terracotta façade and red Spanish tile roof. The Cinderella closed in the mid-1970s and was demolished a few years later.

- Clave

  Basic Latin rhythm, a five-stroke pattern used for temporal organization of Afro-Cuban music. It is present in a variety of genres including Abakuá music, rumba, songa, son, mambo, salsa, songo, timba and Afro-Cuban jazz.

- Club Industry

  Venue that hosted top-shelf music performances in Pontiac, Michigan. It opened in the early 1990s and is now closed.

- Clutch Cargo's

  Short-lived Detroit concert venue (punk club) on West Elizabeth Street (Park/Woodward) that opened in 1981 and closed less than a year later. Performances were staged in the second floor ballroom. Also known as City Club, it is not to be confused with Leland City Club on Bagley.

- Cobb's Corner Bar

  Detroit bar at 4201 Cass Avenue serving as a casual spot for drinks and as a biker hangout when it opened in 1970. It became an up-and-coming jazz destination in 1979 but lost momentum in 1980 when one of the owners was shot and killed in his next door apartment in what is believed to have been a drug related incident. The place closed a few years later and didn't reopen until 2018, sharing its space with Willis Street Gallery.

- comping

  Playing musical accompaniment, especially in jazz or blues.

- contrafact

  A musical work based on a prior work. The term is from classical music as early as the parody mass and *In Nomine* of the 16th century, having only been applied to jazz since the 1970s and still not used commonly. In jazz, contrafact is a composition consisting of a melody overlaid on a familiar harmonic structure. It can also be explained as the use of borrowed chord progressions.

- Dan Lewis & Friends

  See Chapter 4: Elusive Expectations, section "Dan Lewis & Friends." An 11-18-piece group that performed hybrid pop and jazz from 1990 to 2014 at venues that included smooth jazz festivals coordinated by Alexander Zonjic, the Magic Bag, Metro Music Cafe, a festival downtown called Dally in the Alley, Baker's Keyboard Lounge, Sully's in Dearborn, the Montreux-Detroit Jazz Festival (now the Detroit Jazz Festival), Industry in Pontiac, and a venue called Arts, Beats & Eats. Members included Dan Lewis, Al Ayoub, Bob Tye, Gary Schunk, Leonard King, Larry Fratangelo, Jack Dryden, Walter White, Walt Sczymanski, Russ Miller, Ron Kischuk,

Michael Marsac, Scott Peterson, Danny Taylor, Chris McKee, Diane Mathis and John Dunn.

- DB's Club

  Nightclub and music venue in the Hyatt Regency Hotel, Dearborn, Michigan. Many well known performers have played here including Tony Bennett, Della Reese, Lou Rawls, Jose' Feliciano, James Brown, Tina Turner, Buddy Rich and His Orchestra, Ricky Nelson, Jerry Lee Lewis and The Temptations.

- Dummy George's

  The jazz club was located at 10320 West McNichols Road, Detroit, where some of the finest international acts were hosted including singer Jean Carne, organist Jimmy Smith and trumpeter-flugelhorn player Art Farmer.

- Eastown Theatre

  2,500-seat facility at 8041 Harper on the East side of Detroit that opened as a movie theater in 1931 and was converted to a rock music venue in 1967. Performances included Faces, Fleetwood Mac, Steppenwolf, Cream, Pink Floyd and the Amboy Dukes. Alice Cooper (1997) said of the Eastown: "The best audience in the world... Any other city, people went home from work and put on their Levis and black leather jackets for a concert. In Detroit they came from work... those were pure rock'n'roll times." The Eastown later became an adult movie theater, then a site for raves (organized dance parties), and later was obtained by a church group. The building was eventually abandoned and was destroyed by fire in 2010. It was demolished in 2015.

- Ethel's Cocktail Lounge

  Detroit blues club and "dive bar" that was located at 7341 Mack Avenue. Its heyday was from the early 1970s to the early 1980s. Acts included the Ike and Tina Turner Revue, B.B. King and other notables. Urban legend has it that Ethel was a loan shark's girlfriend and that she dumped him for another man.

- The Fillmore Detroit

  Multi-use entertainment venue known as the State Theatre for most of its history. It was built in 1925 in the Detroit Theatre District on Woodward Avenue. The Detroit Music Awards are held here annually. It is on the National Register of Historic Places.

- Fort Shelby Hotel

  Historic Detroit hotel built in 1917 near Fort Street Union Depot on West Lafayette Boulevard at First Street. The hotel nightclub hosted top local talent and international jazz. Renovated in 2007, it is now a Hilton DoubleTree Suites hotel.

- Fortune Records

  Family owned (Jack and Devora Brown), independent record label in Detroit MI 1946-1995. The label specialized in R&B, blues, soul and doo-wop but also released some pop, big band, hillbilly, gospel, rock and roll and polka records. Original releases began to decrease after 1972.

- Grand Riviera Theater

  Italian Renaissance structure located at 9222 Grand River Avenue, built in 1925 as a cinema. It was Detroit's first atmospheric theater, using interior design to create a sense of being outdoors in a garden. In 1957, it was converted to a stage theater. In 1960, due to competition from the Fisher Theater, the Grand Riviera became a venue for music concerts until it closed in the mid-1970s. The structure deteriorated and was demolished in 1996.

- Grande Ballroom

  Historic rock' n roll mecca (Detroit's Rock 'n' Roll Palace) at 8952 Grand River Avenue, built in 1909 and closed in 1972. It was originally used for retail businesses on the first floor with a large dance hall upstairs (1929) renowned for its hardwood dance floor. It became a rock venue in 1966 when it was acquired by Dearborn high school teacher and local DJ Russ Gibb who envisioned a place for teenagers and the new psychedelic music, working collaboratively with John Sinclair. The MC5 recorded their live debut album here. Detroit music natives and national and international artists performed here including avant-garde jazz performances by John Coltrane and Sun Ra as well as future Rock and Roll Hall of Famers too numerous to mention. The Grande is memorialized in the 2012 Emmy award winning film "'Louder Than Love," considered the greatest untold story in rock'n'roll history. The location was added to the National Register of Historic Places in 2018.

- Greenwich Village

  Tree-lined neighborhood that was the epicenter of the 1960s counterculture movement in New York City. It is now filled with cafes, bars and restaurants. Stage play theaters and jazz clubs are found here amid brownstones.

- Guaguancó (wah-wahn-koh)

  Sub-genre of Cuban rumba, combining percussion, voices and dance and having two main styles, Havana and Matanzas. Rumba was traditionally performed in Cuba's streets and courtyards by poor workers of African descent. Wooden boxes were used as drums, replaced by congas in the early 20th century. Guaguancó percussion uses three conga drummers (lowest is tumba, middle is tres dos, highest is quinto), claves (hand-held wood dowels that make a bright clicking sound) played by a narrative singer, guagua (hollowed piece of bamboo) and maraca. Other instruments might include spoons, palitos (wooden sticks striking the side of the drum) and tables and walls played like drums. Guanguancó also refers to a dance of competition between a male and a female.

- Harpos Concert Theatre

  Originally a 1930s cinema, the music venue is located at 14238 Harper Avenue, Detroit. It became a disco club in the mid-70s and later was transformed into a venue for live heavy metal and industrial rock performances.

- Impact Records

  Considered to be one of Detroit's finest record labels of the 1960s, existing from 1965 to 1967 and leaving its mark on Detroit music. Impact recorded and produced artists that included Mickey Denton, The Shades of Blue, Duke Browner Orchestra, The Lollipops and Edwin Starr. The studio didn't survive the 1967 riots.

- Lincoln Park Theater

  Opened as a movie theater on Fort Street in Lincoln Park, a Detroit suburb, in the 1940s. It became a rock club where performers including Bob Seger, the Amboy Dukes and the MC5 played in the mid-1970s.

- The Livingroom

  A prominent Detroit teen dance club where live rock'n'roll and blues were played in the 1960s.

- *A Love Supreme*

  Album that jazz saxophonist John Coltrane recorded in one session in 1964 with his quartet at the time consisting of himself, pianist McCoy Tyner, bassist Jimmy Garrison and drummer Elvin Jones. It was released on Impulse! Records in 1965 and became one of Coltrane's best selling albums as well as one of his most critically acclaimed. The album is considered a masterpiece, one of the greatest albums ever recorded.

- Magic Bag

  Music venue that hosts live performance art, including comedy and tribute bands, in a quirky atmosphere on Woodward Avenue in the Detroit suburb of Ferndale.

- Merengue

  A rhythmic style, rooted in Africa, that came to life in the Dominican Republic. It is based on a repeating five-beat pattern called quintillo (merengue quintuplet), its signature rhythm figure. It is a New World musical style rooted in Old World traditions. Merengue also refers to dancing with merengue music, using long and short stiff-legged steps.

- Metro Music Café

  Dance bar, restaurant and live music venue in Royal Oak, Michigan where jazz acts were hosted during the early 1990s. It is now closed.

- Michigan Palace, a.k.a. Michigan Theater, a.k.a. Michigan Building

  Built on the site of the small garage on Bagley Avenue where Henry Ford created his first automobile, the Renaissance Revival building was constructed in 1925. It has appeared in several movies and has hosted many concerts including Iggy Pop and the Stooges, The New York Dolls, Aerosmith, Bachman Turner Overdrive, Kiss and Blue Oyster Cult. When Iggy Pop and the Stooges played their final gig in 1974, a local motorcycle gang that had been baited by Iggy in a radio interview showed up at the show. When the band took the stage, they were bombarded with broken glass, beer bottles, containers of urine and shovels. Iggy was injured that night. The venue ceased operations in 1976. It currently is known as the Michigan Building and contains a bar, restaurant, retail space, office space, a parking garage and shared co-working space.

- Montreux-Detroit International Jazz Festival (now the Detroit Jazz Festival)

  It began in 1980 in partnership with the highly regarded international jazz festival in Montreux, Switzerland. In 1991, the festival merged with Detroit's Music Hall Center for the Performing Arts and has since acquired philanthropic and corporate support. It is managed by the Detroit International Jazz Festival Foundation and is the largest free jazz festival in the world.

- Montuno

  The word has several meanings related to Cuban music. Translated literally, it means "from the mountain," Son Montuno referring to the older type played in mountainous, rural areas of Cuba. It might also derive from the Spanish word *montura* meaning "the saddle," the rhythm being similar to the sound of a horse's hooves. The word may be used in reference to the final section of a song-based composition, in this sense merely a part of a piece of music in the form of a syncopated piano vamp. Montuno rhythm is frequently at the heart of Cuban dance music.

- Morey Baker's Showplace Lounge

  1960s cutting edge scene for soul, R&B and jazz located on Livernois between Six Mile and Seven Mile Roads in Detroit. The legacy and importance of this music venue, to artists in particular, is showcased in the documentary "Hot Coffey in the D: Burnin' at Morey Baker's Showplace Lounge," titled after an album by Detroit guitarist Dennis Coffey released in 2017. The venue is now closed.

- The Palladium

Former movie theater and Detroit area rock'n'roll concert venue located in Birmingham, Michigan. It operated at full tilt in the early 1970s with performances by Rod Steward and Faces, Tony Williams and Lifetime featuring John McLaughlin and Larry Young.

- Rapa House

After-hours location established by Ernest and LaJune Rodgers for the purpose of providing Detroit musicians with a spot for impromptu jam sessions. It was then operated by their son, Ernie Rodgers, Jr., Detroit jazz musician, educator and coach. The Rapa House heyday was in the 1970s when sessions began at 2:00 a.m., allowing musicians to arrive following their paid gigs.

- Raven Gallery

Live folk, blues and comedy venue at 29101 Greenfield Road, Southfield, Michigan. The venue's heyday was in the 1960s. It closed approximately in the early 1980s.

- riff

A melodic phrase (ostinato) that supports a solo improvisation in jazz, repeated throughout a composition, sometimes varied slightly or transposed to a different pitch. As it relates to rhythm, it's a short, repetitive pattern.

- The Roostertail

  Event and entertainment complex built on the banks of the Detroit River in 1958. The facility has much nostalgia including remaining open through the race riots of the 1960s, family feuds and city financial turmoil. It has hosted some of the biggest names in music history.

- Santeria, a.k.a. Regla de Ocha, a.k.a. Lucumi'

  Pantheistic Afro-Cuban religion based on beliefs and customs of the West African Yorubaland (cultural region of Nigeria) people, incorporating elements of Catholicism. It developed in Cuba between the 16th and 19th centuries through syncretism between Yoruban religion and Roman Catholic Christianity when enslaved Africans from Nigeria and Benin mingled with the Spaniards who owned plantations. Followers believe one god created the universe and the world is overseen by lesser divine beings called orishas, similar to Greek gods, representing forces of nature and having certain human characteristics, Yemaya' being the orisha of the sea and motherhood.

- scat (vocal percussive scat, also called scat singing)

  Jazz vocal style that employs emotive, onomatopoeic (formation of a word from an associated sound such as flippity-flop or sizzle) and nonsense syllables. It is wordless vocal improvisation in which the singer makes up rhythms and melodies using the voice as an instrument. Melodic lines are often variations on scale and arpeggio fragments, stock patterns and riffs. Choice of syllable influences pitch articulation, coloration and resonance as well as differentiating jazz singers' personal styles. Betty Carter was inclined to use sounds like "louie-ooie-la-la-la," whereas Sarah Vaughn preferred "shoo-doo-shoo-bee-ooo-bee."

- Seventh Avenue South

  New York City jazz club in Greenwich Village at 21 Seventh Avenue and Leroy Street, Manhattan that operated from 1977 to 1987. Founded by jazz notables the Brecker brothers Michael (1950-2007, tenor saxophonist) and Randy (trumpeter). The club, a hot spot for the jazz, fusion and studio scene, hosted greats such as John Scofield, Miles Davis, Mike Stern, Wynton Marsalis, Hiram Bullock, David Sanborn, Junior Cook, Kazumi Watanabe and Jaco Pastorius. Albums were recorded in the club.

- SoHo

  New York City neighborhood with fancy chain stores and high-end art galleries, known for its elegant cast iron facades and cobblestone streets. It also boasts gourmet eating spots and nightlife hot spots. Street vendors are a daytime attraction, selling everything from jewelry to original artwork.

- Spirit of Harmony Foundation

  Non-profit organization founded by Todd Rundgren to support the moral imperative of music education and music performance for youth. It focuses on instrument-based music education beginning at as early an age as possible and is based on the concept that music is an integral element of the human experience.

- Strata Concert Gallery

  Detroit concert venue at 46 Selden Street. In 2018, five two-track master tapes of the Charles Mingus Quartet, recorded here during a week-long residency in 1973, were discovered in the care of Hermine Brooks, widow of innovative Detroit drummer Roy Brooks. The recordings have been described as "electrifying." Strata Gallery has been closed for many years.

- Sweet Basil Jazz Club

  Located in New York City's Greenwich Village, the club opened in 1974 and closed in 2001. It was one of the most prominent jazz clubs in the city, and many jazz albums were recorded there.

- The 20 Grand (The Twenty Grand)

  Located at the intersection of 14th Street and Warren Avenue, Detroit's most celebrated night club opened in 1953, built for Detroit radio personality "Frantic" Ernie Durham. It was destroyed by fire in 1958 but later transformed into a multiplex facility for Black audiences, becoming the place to be for "soul" happenings. The first floor was a bowling alley with fireside lounge and jazz room. The upper level was a banquet and cabaret hall (could seat 1,200 people), and it also contained the Driftwood Lounge where performances took place including The Supremes, Chuck Jackson, Parliament-Funkadelic, Stevie Wonder, Mick Jagger and B.B. King. The 20 Grand closed in the mid-1970s.

- United Sound Studios (now United Sound Systems)

  Historic Detroit recording studio located at 5840 2nd Street. Over the past seventy years, many popular music artists have recorded here including blues legend John Lee Hooker (recorded "Boogie Chillen'" here), funk groups such as Funkadelic, Dizzy Gillespie, Johnnie Ray, Jackie Wilson, Dan Shafer and Alberta Adams. United Sound is the site of the first recording for the Tamla label in 1959 before Berry Gordy started Motown Records. Studio ownership changed in 2009, and it was reopened in 2014. In 2015, it was designated a local historic site by the City of Detroit.

- Village Vanguard

  New York City jazz club on Seventh Avenue South in Greenwich Village that opened in 1935 for folk music and beat poetry with some stand-up comedy, becoming primarily a jazz venue in 1957. It hosts many renowned jazz musicians and is the oldest operating jazz club in the city. Jazz greats who have played here include Miles Davis, Horace Silver, Thelonius Monk (launched his career), Gerry Mulligan, Jimmy Giuffre, Sonny Rollins, Anita O'Day, Charles Mingus, Bill Evans (a regular), Stan Getz and Carmen Rae.

- Watts Club Mozambique

  Detroit jazz and R&B venue located at Fenkell and Cherrylawn. It opened in 1969, named in honor of the African country that was fighting for independence. When revenue from jazz performances did not pay the bills, the owner (Cornelius Watts) converted the night spot into a male strip club. It was permanently closed after a fire damaged it in 2015.

- West Village

  Area in New York City with designer boutiques, trendy restaurants, quaint cobblestone streets and Federal-style townhouses. Notable spots are Village Vanguard, a jazz club, and Stonewall Bar, site of the 1969 riots that began the gay rights movement.

- The Wisdom Tooth, a.k.a. Plum Street Coffee House

  Detroit folk coffee house located at 925 Plum Street at the corner of 5ᵗʰ Street where they also hosted after-hours jazz. The Plum Street area was known as Detroit's Art Community, but it was primarily a hippie haunt where various "head shops" sold posters, incense, clothing, and paraphernalia. The Wisdom Tooth was burned during the 1967 riots and never reopened.

- Your Mustache Lounge

  Small live music venue in the style of a listening room located on Ford Road in Dearborn, Michigan. It is no longer in operation.

Ending Note

During the sound check for a performance that includes pianist McCoy Tyner, it's apparent the mix isn't right. The other instruments drown the piano. Even though we're in the audience, Roy Brooks demands that it be fixed. The atmosphere is tense during an urgent sound adjustment. As we're standing by, Roy whispers, "It's so quiet in here, you can hear 'em listen."

Dan Lewis and co-writer Sally Sulfaro
Photo by Pennie Spence

Author Bios

Dan Lewis

In spite of being confined to a wheelchair from birth, Dan Lewis has shared stages, and more importantly friendships, with Detroit greats and international music icons including Al Jarreau, Edgar Winter, Elvin Jones, Andy Newmark, Bennie Maupin and Dave Liebman. His life has been filled with uphill struggles to master percussion, having to compromise and settle for hand percussion with the guidance and support of other musicians. His primary genre is jazz, but he is also steeped in blues, R&B and American standards.

In addition to being a performing musician, Dan is a music aficionado—a pre-eminent music historian who has taken part in numerous radio interviews and panel discussions. He owns an impressive collection of recordings. The sound or mention of a tune triggers not only memories and stories from Dan but also the year of release, the label, the songwriter, the arranger, the producer and other recordings of the same tune. He is a rolling Motown compendium, a Who's Who of Motown and way beyond that territory, including recording studios and labels. As such, Dan does not kneel at the foot of the great Motown monument but rather notes its shortcomings with regard to artists and roots while acknowledging its international and sociocultural reach.

Dan's life story is a collage of sounds, people and places that evoke tears, laughter and nostalgia. Written with author Sally Sulfaro, his autobiography contains a music aficionado's perspectives on the art and the business as well as his thoughts on life, spirituality and coping. Some perceive Dan as a sage, and he truly is—but those who know him well also realize that he's no saint. On the pages of *Compared to What? Life and Times of a Detroit Musician* readers experience his unvarnished memoirs.

Sally Sulfaro

Sally Sulfaro is a retired nurse executive, leadership coach, healthcare systems consultant and a former vice president of operations with a national physician management company. She was drawn to writing after the death of her son, Detroit rock musician, author and poet Abe Sulfaro. His unpublished manuscript, the dark novel *The Antiheroes: Treatise of a Lost Soul*, was left in her hands when he died of pancreatic cancer in 2014. It has since been published as well as a collection of his prose, song lyrics and quotes in *Memoirs de Nocturne: An Anthology.* Since then, Sally has authored the novel *Co-eternals: A Story of Entangled Consciousness*, a companion book to *The Antiheroes*; has co-written *Compared to What? Life and Times of a Detroit Musician*, the autobiography of Detroit percussionist Dan Lewis; and is currently working on a stage play based on *The Antiheroes*.

Made in the USA
Monee, IL
24 December 2021

86715865R00157